Welcome to
Windows 10
The Complete Manual

The Start menu is back!
Windows 8 was a massive departure from the
operating system we all knew and loved, but
Windows 10 takes the best parts of Windows 8,
and merges them elegantly with the best parts
of Windows 7 to create Microsofts' most loved
OS to date. With the introduction of Cortana, your
new voice assistant, and with the brand-new
web browser, Edge, Windows has never been a
stronger platform! Enjoy the book.

Windows 10
The Complete Manual

Imagine Publishing Ltd
Richmond House
33 Richmond Hill
Bournemouth
Dorset BH2 6EZ
☎ +44 (0) 1202 586200
Website: www.imagine-publishing.co.uk
Twitter: @Books_Imagine
Facebook: www.facebook.com/ImagineBookazines

Publishing Director
Aaron Asadi

Head of Design
Ross Andrews

Production Editor
Jasmin Snook

Senior Art Editor
Greg Whitaker

Designer
Phil Martin

Photographer
James Sheppard

Printed by
William Gibbons, 26 Planetary Road, Willenhall, West Midlands, WV13 3XT

Distributed in the UK, Eire & the Rest of the World by
Marketforce, 5 Churchill Place, Canary Wharf, London, E14 5HU
Tel 0203 787 9060 www.marketforce.co.uk

Distributed in Australia by
Gordon & Gotch Australia Pty Ltd, 26 Rodborough Road, Frenchs Forest, NSW, 2086 Australia
Tel +61 2 9972 8800 www.gordongotch.com.au

Windows 10 The Complete Manual Second Edition © 2016 Imagine Publishing Ltd

ISBN 9781785462948

IMAGINE
PUBLISHING

Contents
What you can find inside the bookazine

You can get Cortana to
tell you a joke, by simply
saying "Hey Cortana, tell
me a joke!"

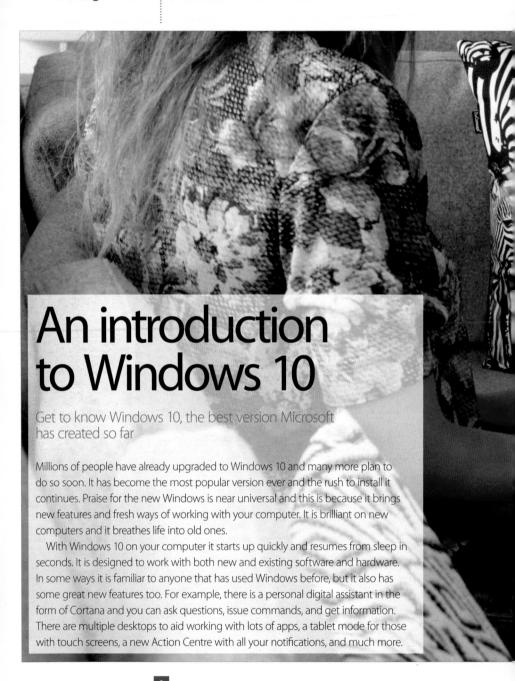

An introduction to Windows 10

Get to know Windows 10, the best version Microsoft has created so far

Millions of people have already upgraded to Windows 10 and many more plan to do so soon. It has become the most popular version ever and the rush to install it continues. Praise for the new Windows is near universal and this is because it brings new features and fresh ways of working with your computer. It is brilliant on new computers and it breathes life into old ones.

With Windows 10 on your computer it starts up quickly and resumes from sleep in seconds. It is designed to work with both new and existing software and hardware. In some ways it is familiar to anyone that has used Windows before, but it also has some great new features too. For example, there is a personal digital assistant in the form of Cortana and you can ask questions, issue commands, and get information. There are multiple desktops to aid working with lots of apps, a tablet mode for those with touch screens, a new Action Centre with all your notifications, and much more.

The Start menu

The Start menu is back in Windows 10, as it was one of the most requested features. If you have upgraded from Windows 7 you will find some familiar features, but also some exciting new ones too. It is a fusion of the old Start menu and the Windows 8 Start screen, and it incorporates the best features of both, enabling you to access apps and settings and faster.

Fig 1 After briefly disappearing in Windows 8, the Start menu is back in Windows 10

Your most-used applications are listed on the left side where they are easily accessed (Fig 1). One click opens the Start menu and another starts your favourite app. The All apps link is similar to the All programs link on the old Start menu, which makes it familiar for people upgrading older PCs.

The Start menu has Windows 8-style tiles. They are not just menu links to software and they can be live (Fig 2). This enables them to display snippets of information and the Calendar app can show your next appointment, the Mail app can show a recent email, and so on.

Live tiles are a clever way to keep you updated with the important things that are happening in your life without you having to open multiple apps.

Fig 2 The Start menu is bigger and better. It is expandable and has live tiles

Updated apps

The Windows Store and apps were new to Windows 8 and they are also in Windows 10. However, they have changed and unlike the previous version of the operating system, they do not take over the whole screen and they run in a window on the desktop just like regular software (Fig 3). This makes working with desktop software and Windows Store apps much better than it used to be and it is also easier than ever to run two, three or more apps side by side. All of your favourite apps can be kept open in Windows on the desktop and this is a great new feature that will make you more productive.

In addition to running in a window, the bundled apps have had a makeover and feature update too, and they are now better and more practical.

Take the Mail app, for example. It has a new interface that looks very smart and is easy to use. It also supports touch too, for those people with touch screens, and swiping left or right across emails in your inbox enables actions to be performed, such as deleting or archiving. The new apps are more fun, more useful and easier than ever.

Fig 3 Apps now run in their own window and several of them can run simultaneously at the same time

Fig 4 Multiple desktops are available, allowing your apps to spread across them

Windows 10 helps you work and play

Increase productivity Use the Mail app to deal with incoming messages quickly and easily, and use the Calendar app to schedule appointments and organise both your work and leisure time.

Enhance your lifestyle There are many lifestyle apps in the Windows Store and they include fashion magazines, horoscopes, beauty, hair and makeup, diaries, journals and much more. Explore the Store.

Entertain yourself and family Windows comes with several entertainment apps, such as Films & TV and Groove. There are many more, such as Netflix for movies and TV, and game apps.

Multiple desktops

More people are using laptop computers these days and there are also new types of computers, such as PC-laptop hybrids like the Microsoft Surface. All have small screens and this makes working with more than a couple of applications or windows awkward. With windows stacked on top of each other it is hard to find the one you want. Windows 10 now incorporates multiple desktops to enhance working on small screens.

With a swipe and tap, or a couple of mouse clicks, extra desktops can be created and this enables applications to have their own screen (Fig 4). It makes working with your computer simpler and you could edit a WordPad document on one screen, explore the web with Edge on a second and browse holiday snaps with the Photos app on a third. You'll get more done with Windows 10.

A new Action Centre has several functions. One is to provide a central place for viewing notifications and important messages, another is to provide quick-action buttons, such as turning your Bluetooth capabilities on or off, changing the screen brightness, setting quiet hours that stop notifications, and so on. Action Centre simplifies many functions and makes sure you will not miss anything important.

Essential PC accessories

Smartphone

Any Android phone or iPhone is a great Windows accessory. Get OneDrive, Word, Excel, Outlook, and Groove, then access documents, photos, music and videos on your PC

Wireless keyboard and mouse

This top-of-the-range keyboard and mouse is wireless with a two-year battery life and one-click access to Cortana, OneNote and virtual desktops. The Microsoft Wireless Desktop 900 costs £50/$50

Printer

HP has many great printers and this one is a budget model for home users that offers wireless printing, scanning and copying for just £50/$80

External speakers

PCs rarely have good speakers for music and movies, but luckily Logitech has a good range. The Z533 is a great 2.1 sound system for £79/$100

External USB drive

This external USB drive from Western Digital comes in sizes up to 5TB. It is perfect for backups and Windows 10's File History. Priced from £65/$89 for 2TB

4K Monitor

If you need a new monitor to match your new operating system, this model offers 4K resolution, which displays sharp images for just £538/$1,000 for the 28-inch version

Cortana

Fig 5 Talk to Cortana and ask anything, such as converting pounds to dollars

Cortana is an artificial intelligence character in the *Halo* games and Microsoft has incorporated her into Windows 10 as a personal digital assistant. Cortana is one of the standout features of the new operating system and has many functions. One of these is the voice recognition and you can now speak to your computer. Just like on *Star Trek*! Cortana answers questions and carries out actions (Fig 5). Ask "Will I need an umbrella tomorrow?" and Cortana answers by showing a weather forecast. Say "Make an appointment to see Bob tomorrow at 1pm" and Cortana adds it to the calendar and creates a reminder so you don't forget (Fig 6). It is brilliant for busy people.

When Cortana cannot answer directly, a browser window is opened to show search results from Bing. This enables subjects to be researched easily and with minimal typing. You can just start from a spoken query. Cortana can be permanently on, ready to answer questions and perform actions. All you have to do is say "Hey, Cortana". Cortana doubles up as a computer search facility and you can click in the search box and type whatever you are looking for, such as a file or Windows setting.

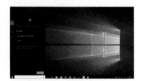

Fig 6 Cortana can perform actions, such as making a new Calendar appointment for example

Top Windows apps

Panda Free Antivirus Replace Windows Defender with better antivirus software such as Panda Internet Security (**pandasecurity.com**).

Office Online Office Online (**office.com**) is free using the Edge browser on OneDrive and it lets you use Word, Excel and others.

EaseUS Todo Backup Free Back up everything on your PC's disk to an external USB disk drive so you never lose a file (**todo-backup.com**).

Apple iTunes iTunes (**apple.com**) is essential if you have an iPhone or iPad, but even if you don't, it is a useful music and movie player and store.

VLC Player This is a media player that can cope with just about any type of media file and it also plays DVD movies on disc too (**videolan.org**).

Ashampoo Burning Studio Free Burn CDs, DVDs and Blu-ray discs to backup photos and create movie and music discs (**ashampoo.com/trips**).

IObit Uninstaller Use this to clean up after programs when removing them (**iobit.com**). It's more powerful than Programs and Features.

ZoneAlarm Free Firewall Windows Firewall is okay, but some others offer superior security, such as ZoneAlarm Free Firewall (**zonealarm.com**).

Paint.NET Paint is a simple Windows image editor, but Paint.NET (**getpaint. net**) is a powerful and feature-packed photo editor with excellent tools.

"Cortana can be permanently on, ready to answer questions. All you have to do is say 'Hey, Cortana'"

Set up your PC

Follow our quick-start guide to setting up a new Windows 10 PC or upgrading an old one

1 **Connect to Wi-Fi** Windows needs an internet connection and it will use the Wi-Fi to look for wireless networks to connect to. If you are not online, click the network button at the right side of the taskbar and a list of available networks is displayed (Fig 1). Make sure Windows is connected to your own network and not a neighbour's. Click the Wi-Fi network to connect or disconnect from it.

2 **Access your account** Everything in Windows 10 works better if you have a Microsoft account, such as an **Outlook.com** email address. If you did not sign in to Windows with a Microsoft account, go to Start>Settings>Accounts. Below the Your picture graphic is a button to capture or select a photo to use. To sign in to Windows 10 with a Microsoft account, click the Sign in… link (Fig 2).

Fig 1 Click the network icon to connect to Wi-Fi

3 **Create an account** Many features in Windows 10 do not fully work without a Microsoft account and if you already have one, such as an Outlook.com email account, enter the email address and password here. If you do not have an account or if you want a new one, click the link to create one. It will activate OneDrive and several other features in Windows 10 that are very useful.

4 **Check Action Centre** At the right side of the taskbar just before the clock is an Action Centre button. Click it to access a collection of useful buttons for turning features on or off, accessing settings and more (Fig 3). It displays important messages and these can be anything from asking you to run a virus scan using Windows Defender, verifying your identity, or the latest email messages.

Fig 2 Check the settings in your account

5 **Verify your identity** At some point during the setup, you may be asked to verify your identity. This is part of the improvements to security for Windows 10. If a mobile phone number is associated with your account, Microsoft will send a security code to it and you must type it in (Fig 4). This links your new Windows 10 account with your phone and proves your identity.

6 **Add more users** Are there other people that want to use the computer? A home computer might be accessed by both adults and children. Instead of everyone using the same account, each person can have their own and this contains their personal photos, documents, email, music and so on. Go to Start> Settings>Accounts>Family & other users. There is a button to add a family member. Click it and follow the instructions.

Fig 3 Open the Action Centre to read messages

Find the Get Started app on the Start menu and run it. It's a video guide to Windows 10

Fig 4 Verify your identity to prove who you are

Set up your PC

Fig 5 Select a background in Personalisation

Fig 6 Keep checking for updates and get them all

Fig 7 Make it secure when waking from sleep

7 Set the wallpaper Windows applies default settings to things, such as the background image used on the desktop. The image changes a lot and can be distracting. To select a fixed image, right-click the desktop and select Personalise. Select Background in the Personalisation settings and then select one of the thumbnail pictures (Fig 5) or click Browse to select your own photo.

8 Set the colour The colours used for window borders and for tiles on the Start menu are automatically selected by Windows. If the colour chosen is not to your liking, change it. Right-click the desktop and select Personalise. Select Colours on the left, then set the switch to Off. In the grid of coloured tiles that appears below, click the colour you want to use for the tiles and borders.

9 Install updates Windows 10 is frequently updated and the version you have is out of date. This is perfectly normal. Windows automatically downloads and installs the latest updates, but you can speed things up by going to Start> Settings>Update & Security>Windows Update. Click the Check for updates button. Restart Windows and repeat this until there are no more updates (Fig 6).

10 Wake up options If the computer is idle or if a laptop's lid is closed, it enters Sleep mode. Touch a key or open the lid and it wakes up. The question is, do you want it to be locked with a password or unlocked when it wakes? Go to Start>Settings>Accounts>Sign-in options. Under Require sign in are Never and When PC wakes up from sleep (Fig 7). Requiring a password is more secure.

11 Set up Cortana Cortana needs setting up before it can be used. Click the search box on the taskbar and follow the instructions. There are welcome messages, tips and questions. You might be asked to read a sentence out loud to check that there is a microphone in the computer and that it is working properly. Set up takes no more than a minute and then you can talk to Cortana.

12 Try the apps Many apps have welcome screens that are displayed only once when they are first run. These screens display brief help or usage instructions and sometimes they require you to select settings and options, or to sign in with an account or add an account. Once this is done, the apps then work normally. It it worth spending an hour running each app on the Start menu once (Fig 8).

If you have other devices like a printer or scanner, they can be added in Settings>Devices

Fig 8 Many apps have once-only screens and info

The Start menu and desktop

Your account
Click your photo for a menu with options to log out or view your account

Drag and drop
Click and drag the title bar of a group of tiles to move it elsewhere

Edit the titles
Tiles are organised into groups with titles at the top. Click it to change it

More apps
There are more programs on the computer. Click All apps to see them

Tile options
Right-click a tile for a menu with options to change its size

Expand the menu
Click and drag the right-hand edge of the Start menu to change the size

A guide to the Start menu apps

Mail
Mail is a great email app that can be used with Microsoft, Google and other types of accounts.

Maps
Explore the world with 3D cities in the Maps app. Also get driving directions with the route planner facility.

Cortana
The app tile is an alternative way to access Cortana. Click it and Cortana is ready to answer your questions.

Photos
Browse, view and edit your digital camera or phone photos stored on the computer or on OneDrive.

Weather
Use the Weather app to get an accurate forecast for your local area or for any place in the world.

Groove Music
The Groove app is a music player. Use it to play your own music or Microsoft's streaming music service.

Microsoft Edge
Edge is a brand new, lightweight and fast web browser that is a replacement for the old Internet Explorer.

Store
The Windows Store has everything you need, including software, music, movies and TV. There's free stuff too.

Films & TV
Movies, television shows and series bought in the Store appear in this app. Use it to watch your purchases.

Calendar
Use the Calendar app to look up dates, create appointments and set reminders so you will never miss them.

Skype
Skype enables you to send text messages and photos to friends, and also make voice and video calls.

Xbox
This is for gamers with an Xbox and it keeps you in touch with the community. View friends and Achievements.

How to use Windows 10

This guide will have you using your computer like a pro. Windows 10 is easy!

Windows 10 makes using your computer more fun and more productive. Whether you play games, watch movies, interact on social media websites, or work on your PC, there are features that make it simpler and easier. In this section we will look at some of the basic features of Windows 10 and show how quick it is to get online, customise the Start menu, personalise the look of Windows and more. If you have used an older version of Windows, you will find that features have moved or are accessed in different ways, but once you get used to 10's way of working, it is much better. For example, it is easier than ever to open two apps side by side and to work with both at once, as our guide shows.

Connect to Wi-Fi

1 View available networks Click the network icon at the right side of the task bar to see a list of available Wi-Fi networks.

2 Connect to Wi-Fi Click the Wi-Fi network you want and then click Connect. For a home network, tick Connect automatically.

Shut down Windows

2 Use Start Click the Start menu, Power and then Shut down.

1 Close running programs Check the task bar for running programs before shutting down. Underlined icons that show thumbnails when the mouse hovers over them are running. Click them and quit.

3 Power button action Control Panel settings mean pressing the power button shuts down.

Customise Start Menu

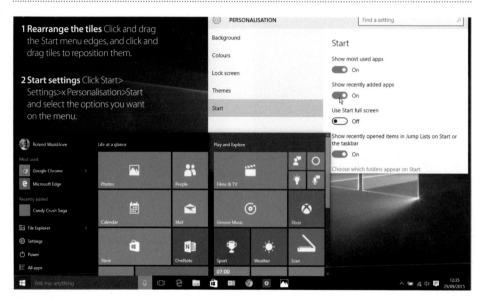

1 Rearrange the tiles Click and drag the Start menu edges, and click and drag tiles to reposition them.

2 Start settings Click Start> Settings>x Personalisation>Start and select the options you want on the menu.

Set wallpaper

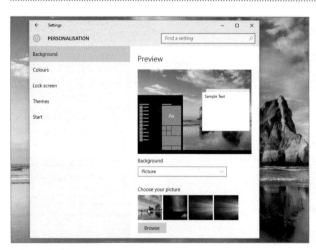

1 Personalisation options Right-click the Windows desktop and then select Personalise on the menu that appears. Settings opens and shows several thumbnail images of desktop backgrounds. Click the one you want to use.

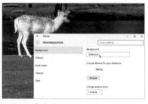

2 Use a slideshow Click the Background menu and select Slideshow to use your photos.

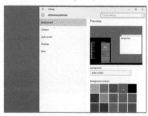

3 Set a colour Select Solid Colour for the Background and click a colour.

Search your PC

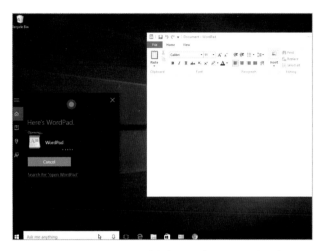

2 Type search terms Click the search box and type filenames to find them.

1 **Use Cortana** Say "Hey Cortana" or click the microphone icon and speak your search. Ask Cortana to open WordPad for example, and it will find it and open it ready to use. It is quick and easy.

3 Search for settings Can't find a setting? Type it into the search box.

Open two apps side by side

2 Rearrange the apps If app windows overlap, drag the titles to reposition.

1 **Open your apps** Opening apps side by side is much easier than it used to be. Just go to the Start menu and open one app, then return and open the second app you want to use.

3 Auto arrange apps Drag each app to the screen edge to resize them.

Pin to Start menu

1 Browse All apps Open the Start menu and click the All apps link at the bottom.

2 Right click menu Right-click your favourite apps and select the option to Pin to Start.

Customise Start screen tiles

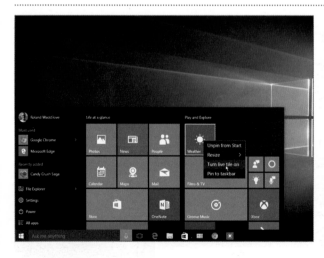

2 Change the size Right-click a tile, select Resize and pick a size.

1 Enable live tiles Start screen and Start menu tiles can show live information, such as weather forecasts, emails, calendar appointments and more. Right-click a tile and select Turn live tile on or off as preferred.

3 Biggest is best Some tiles work really well in their largest size.

Set parental controls

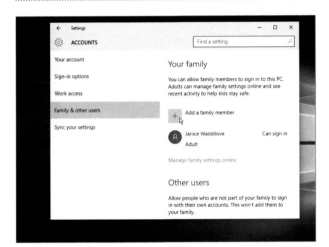

1 Add your family To control what your children can do on the computer, go to Start>Settings>Accounts. Select Family members and then click the plus to add one or more child user accounts.

2 Family settings online Click Manage family settings online and click a child account.

3 Change the settings Click Change settings next to Web Browsing, Games and so on.

Select a theme

1 Personalise your PC
Right-click on the desktop and select Personalise. Select Themes followed by Theme settings.

2 Select a theme
A small collection of themes is displayed here. Just click on one to select it and then use it.

3 Get more themes
Click the 'Get more themes online' link to add even more themes on to your computer.

Create a desktop shortcut

1 Find the item Click File Explorer and find the file you want to create a shortcut for.

2 Send to desktop Right-click it and select Send to>Desktop (create shortcut).

Learn your PC's keyboard

Keyboard shortcuts can greatly speed up your day-to-day Windows 10 usage

Keyboard Shortcuts

Show/hide Desktop

Switch to new virtual desktop

Initiate Cortana

Open Task Manager

Open Windows Explorer

Snap app to top

Quit Metro apps

Minimize all Windows

Windows 10 allows you to snap apps into a 2x2 grid, simply tap 🪟 then the directional arrow

shortcuts

Mail

Reply

 Ctrl + R

Show all messages

Ctrl + ⇧ + A

Clear formatting

 **Ctrl** + **Space bar**

Show only unread messages

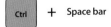 **Ctrl** + ⇧ + U

Microsoft Edge

Go to next page

Alt + →

Find on a page

Ctrl + F

Open an InPrivate browsing window

 **Ctrl** + ⇧ + P

Open the Tools menu

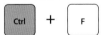 **Alt** + T

File Explorer

Show subfolders under selected folder

Num Lock + *

Display the preview pane

Alt + P

Create a new folder

 **Ctrl** + ⇧ + N

Open a new Explorer window

 **Ctrl** + N

Getting started

Take your first steps by getting to know the interface and the apps

Fig 1 There are new ways of working with Windows, including browsing with Edge and Settings

Fig 2 Whether you play games or work on your PC, it is now easier to use than ever

Windows 10 contains some new features and clever ways to help you work faster and get more out of your computer. Some of the features will be familiar to anyone that has used a Windows computer, but there are also new features and ways of working too.

The Start menu is familiar, but also different, and it provides new ways to access and organise the software on the computer. The live tiles show important information at a glance and can be configured in whatever arrangement suits you best. Windows 10 enables you to interact with the computer through spoken commands and Cortana is a new assistant that redefines the way you think about doing tasks and getting information. You can also interact with Windows 10 through touch and a pen, which opens up new possibilities, like writing on the screen. There are also improved security features that make using Windows safer.

Desktop

Get to know the Start screen and the apps and menus

Fig 1 Tap the menu button in the top-left corner to open the Start menu

The Start screen that was familiar to Windows 8 users is still in Windows 10 and it can be activated with a couple of mouse clicks. It is designed for computers with touch-enabled screens, such as desktop PCs, laptops, the Microsoft Surface and other tablets, but it can also be used with a mouse too. If the Start screen is not visible, click the Action Centre icon at the right side of the task bar and click the Tablet mode button.

Some features are like Windows 8, but some are new to Windows 10. Bundled apps and Windows Store apps you download appear as tiles and they can be organised into groups. Click a tile to run an app and it fills the screen. You might find this way of working preferable to desktop mode because it keeps you focused on a single app without being distracted by other windows. Right-click a tile for a menu with options to resize them.

Fig 2 Tap the menu button bottom-left to open the All apps listing

Start menu

Explore the new Windows 10 Start menu and access your favourite apps

Windows 10 starts up in desktop mode on desktop computers and laptops, and this provides a familiar environment, but one that has new features too. The Start screen seen in tablet mode is replaced by a Start menu and desktop. The menu contains everything on the Start screen, but it also has some extra features, such as the ability to re-size so it can be wide or narrow.

The tiles can display an icon and text title, but they can also show live information like emails, news headlines, weather reports, stock market information, photos and more. The information displayed depends on the app. Live tiles enable you to see what is new at a glance.

Jump lists
Some apps have a little arrow on the right. Click it and it displays a jump list containing recently accessed files, websites, tasks and other useful items

Live tile menu
Right-click an app tile to display a menu. Choose between showing a static tile with icon and title or a live tile like the weather app shown below

Resize tiles
Many tiles can be displayed in four sizes, although some do not support the largest size. Right-click a tile and select Resize, then one of the sizes

Most-used apps
As you use the computer, Windows takes note of which apps you use the most and it places them in a list here. It makes them even easier to access

Rearrange tiles
This is an example of the largest tile size and the Weather app is showing a mini forecast. Click and drag it to position it elsewhere on the Start menu

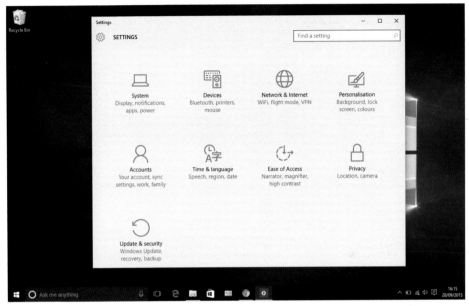

Settings

Configure Windows settings and make it work the way you want it to

The brand new Settings app in Windows 10 (click Start>Settings) enables you to customise the way Windows looks and works. It means that you can personalise it and make it work in a way that best suits the way your work on your computer or the leisure activities it is used for. Simple examples of this are the options to change the desktop background and colours, and the lock screen image. You don't have to accept the default image and colour scheme and you can select your own.

Settings is where you set up devices like printers, scanners, a Bluetooth mouse or keyboard. It provides access to user accounts where you can manager your own, add another person, change permissions and passwords, and more. A privacy section contains controls for setting the amount of information you share, and it enables you to get Windows updates and recover from problems.

Fig 1 Settings are used to customise the hardware, such as various power options, and software

Fig 2 Use Settings to add new hardware to use with Windows and show any devices that are connected

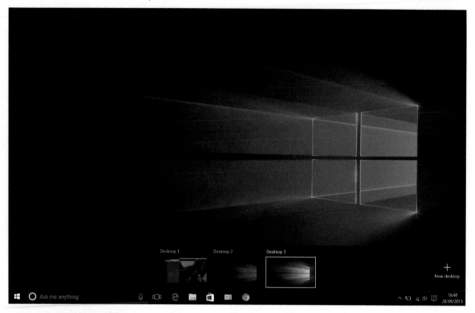

Fig 1 When the screen is cluttered, click Task View and add more desktops

Multiple Desktops

Create multiple virtual desktops and spread your apps out across them

Many people use Windows on small screens such as laptops, and when several apps are open at once, their windows overlap and it is hard to manage. Multiple virtual desktops is the solution and if one screen is not big enough, how about two, three, four or more?

Click the Task View icon just to the right of the search box on the task bar and a plus button at the far right of the screen enables more desktops to be added. They appear as thumbnails just above the task bar and clicking one of them switches to that desktop. This gives you a fresh, empty desktop onto which you can open a window or an app without the clutter and overlap from other apps. Apps can be dragged from one desktop to another to gain more screen space.

Fig 2 Select a desktop thumbnail and drag the apps to another one to move it

Windows Hello

Unlock your computer with a look or a swipe of your finger

Windows Hello is a new way to unlock your computer and it makes it more secure, yet easier to access. This feature means that if your computer has a compatible camera, it can recognise your face and log you in. Alternatively, if your computer has a fingerprint reader, it can be unlocked by swiping a digit over it. What could be simpler than looking at your computer?

First you need to see whether Windows Hello is supported on your computer. If it is, it will appear as an option in Settings>Account>Sign-in options. If there is no suitable camera or fingerprint scanner, you will not see a Windows Hello option.

Accounts settings
Windows Hello is accessed through Settings. Click the Start menu and then select Settings. Click the Accounts category and a list of categories is displayed on the left

Set up a PIN
A PIN code to access your account must be set up before Windows Hello is ready. If you have not already done so, click the button and set a memorable, complex PIN code, like 827363

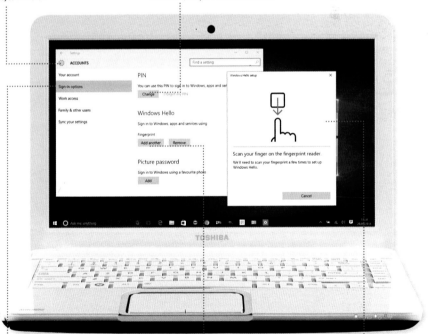

Sign-in options
Select Sign-in options on the left in Accounts. Whenever you change anything to do with your account, you are usually required to enter your password again

Set up for fingerprints
This PC has a fingerprint reader and it can be used by Windows Hello to unlock it instead of entering a password. Click the button to add one or more fingerprints

Add a fingerprint
The fingerprint reader on this PC is a small black bar that you swipe your finger over. You must do this several times to make sure it is read correctly

Snap

Automatically arrange apps and windows on the desktop in a grid pattern

Snap is a not a new feature, but it has been improved in Windows 10. It is easier than ever to rearrange multiple windows on the desktop so that you can see them all without them overlapping. Snap enables apps and windows to be dragged to the left or right side of the screen and dropped. They are automatically re-sized to fill half of the screen. If you want the app on the other side, just hold down the Windows key and press the left or right arrow key. Use Windows plus the up or down arrow to fill the top or bottom half of the screen. Repeat with another window.

Snap settings
Click Start and then Settings. Click the System category and then select the Multi- tasking section to access the settings for the Snap feature. Turn on all the switches

Turn Snap on
Snap is turned on or off with this switch. Not everyone likes this feature and it is possible to accidentally snap apps and windows when moving them. It's your choice

Snap buddies
Most apps can be snapped to the edges of the screen, but not all of them can. Turning this switch on shows the apps that can be snapped as thumbnail images

Sides and corners
Click and drag the title bar of a window to the left or right edge to fill half of the screen. Drag it to the corners to fill one quarter of the screen

Resizing windows
By enabling this option, whenever you choose to resize a snapped window, all adjacent windows will also be automatically rezised

Switch between apps

Switch from one app to another when several are open on the screen

One of the many improvements in Windows 10 is the ability to run multiple apps and to mix them with standard Windows software. You can work with two, three or as many apps as you need. When lots of app windows are open, switching from one to another is not easy because they overlap and become buried under one another.

There are three ways to switch apps and one obvious method is to go to the task bar and let the mouse hover over an icon to display the thumbnail. If it is the right one, then click the icon or thumbnail to bring the app to the front. There are other ways and you can also hold down the 'Alt' key and repeatedly press tab until the right app is selected and then release to switch.

Fig 1 Press Alt+Tab to display app thumbnails and tab to the app you want

Fig 2 Press Windows+Tab to display larger thumbnails and click the app you want

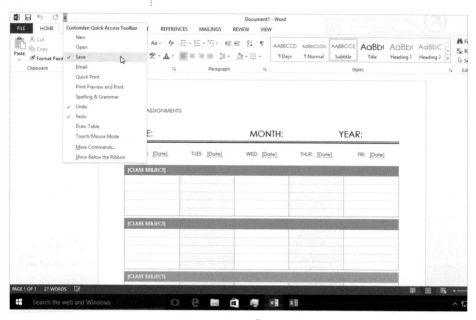

Fig 1 Here we have opened Powerpoint. The options in the tool bar reflect the available tasks

Quick Access toolbar

Find handy shortcuts for common actions

While using Windows 10 you may find yourself performing certain actions on a regular basis, such as saving, printing and using Undo. Windows 10 includes a Quick Access tool bar that puts these tools in one handy location. You'll find it in the top-left corner of an Explorer window or Microsoft program (Fig 1). Click on each icon to perform its action. The tools that are available can be customised by clicking on the arrow on the right-hand end of the row of icons. Tools can then be added or removed by tagging them from the selection that is available (Fig 2). If you're not sure what a certain icon does, you can hover your mouse pointer over it and Windows will display a short explanation. You can also set the tool bar to appear below the ribbon to make it more prominent within your workspace.

Fig 2 Click the arrow to show the list of all the tools that are available. Tag or un-tag them as required

Task Manager

Unlock unresponsive programs and look up real-time system information

The Task Manager displays all of the programs and processes that are currently up and running on your PC. It can also give you an idea of how your computer is working or assist with closing down a program that has stopped responding. If your computer is online, the Task Manager can also display the network status and track how fast the data throughput is.

If you use Windows 10 apps, then the task manager can track individual programs and the length of time used along with how data has been transferred. To access the Task Manager, right-click on the taskbar (at the bottom) and select it from the menu.

Processes
When a program is not responding, you can close it down from the Processes tab. Right-click on the program and select End Task from the menu

Start-up
When booting up Windows, it automatically loads some programs so they are ready to use straight away. Use this tab to manage the list

Tabbed sections
The Task Manager is split up into various sections separated by tabs; click on these to access each aspect

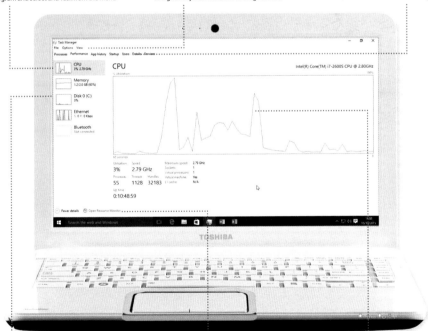

Performance stats
In the Performance section you can click on any of the listed entries to see how they are performing in real-time. You can also adjust how frequently these bar graphs update

Resource Monitor
For an even more comprehensive report on your computer's performance, click the Open Resource Monitor links at the bottom of the window. This is a more advanced tool so tread carefully

Summary view
You can scale the Task Manager window down so that it just shows you the graph. To do so, right-click the graph and select 'Graph Summary view'

Action Centre

Stay in the loop on issues that need to be taken care of

Action Centre is a tool that operates as a hub, allowing you to review recent messages about your computer's status and also troubleshoot any outstanding problems. You'll find it in the lower right area of the task bar, signified by a white speech bubble. Accessing it is done by either left- or right-clicking on the flag and selecting Open Action Centre. If Action Centre locates an issue, a notification will appear in the task bar; clicking it will also open Action Centre.

Problems will have a colour code within the Action Centre: sections marked yellow indicate an issue that requires attention; areas marked in red represent a problem that needs fixing.

Windows Update
Microsoft releases regular updates for Windows that can fix problems or increase security. They may also fix a problem. This link will take you straight to the Windows Update section

Access Control Panel
Being a more technical aspect of Windows, the Action Centre also provides a link to the Control Panel. It can be found in the top-left corner; click it to open the Control Panel

Security and Maintenance
Action Centre is split into two main sections titled Security and Maintenance. Click the arrows to the far right of these titles to expand these sections

Troubleshoot a problem
You may be aware of an issue that is not registering with the Action Centre. Use the Troubleshooting option to pinpoint this issue and search for a possible fix

Turn off messages
If you've had enough of Action Centre's persistent messaging, you can use the built-in options to minimise or switch off these messages

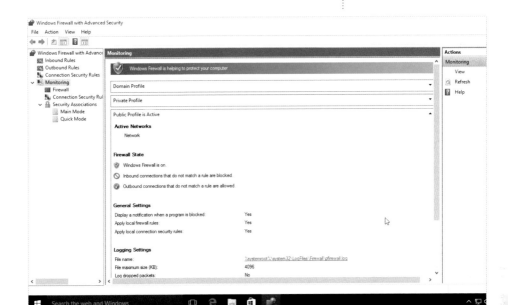

Windows Firewall

Protect yourself from unwanted intrusions with the Windows Firewall

In basic terms, a firewall is a security measure that prevents malware and hackers from getting access to your PC. Windows Firewall is included when you install Windows 10. It is activated by default and for the most part shouldn't require adjustment. You can install an alternative should you wish, but it is recommended to only have one firewall running at a time otherwise conflicts may arise.

Access Windows Firewall by pressing the Start button, typing 'Windows Firewall' and selecting it from the results. An overview screen will show which networks you're connected to and whether Firewall is operating (Fig 1). The Advanced Settings section is used for allowing certain programs and apps through the firewall (Fig 2).

Fig 1 The overview screen includes info on network security and shows whether Windows Firewall is turned on

Fig 2 Click 'Allow an app through' to view a checklist of all the programs not affected by Firewall

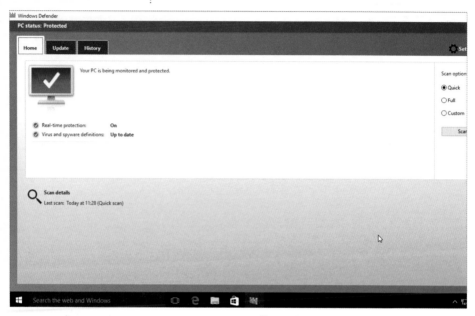

Fig 1 Windows Defender can handle updates by itself or you can choose to do it manually

Windows Defender

Get to grips with the default Windows spyware protection tool

Windows 10 has its own anti-spyware tool: Windows Defender. With it activated, Windows will notify you when spyware or other unwanted software attempts to install itself on your PC. By default, it will keep itself updated with the latest definitions (Fig 1). To open Windows Defender, select the 'Windows' icon and type 'Defender', then select it from the search results. Windows Defender offers real-time protection, but you can request a scan via the buttons on the far right (Fig 2). There are also tabs that take you to each section of the program. Should you ever install an alternative anti-spyware program, Windows Defender will automatically deactivate itself in order to prevent clashes and system issues.

Fig 2 In the Settings section you can scan any external drives and even toggle real-time protection

Disk Management

Organise the partitions that are set up on your hard drive

Disk Management is a slightly more advanced aspect of Windows 10. With it you can set out the partitions of your hard drive to fit your own needs. Partitions are separate sections of your hard drive which will appear as separately labelled drives within Windows 10. Some users like to install Windows on one partition but keep their documents and files on a separate partition.

To open Disk Management, right-click on the Windows icon in the lower left corner and select it from the menu, there are multiple other ways to open it, but this is arguably the quickest way. Once opened, the program will show you a diagram of your hard drive.

Partitions and drives
This section lists your drives along with some details on their status/ role and some basic storage stats. You can right-click any drive to access the drive tools

Extend/shrink volumes
You may find that you need to adjust the sizes of your partitions based on your needs. Use these tools to increase or reduce the size of the selected partition

Visual representation
Here you can see how your partitions are arranged with your hard drive. As with the upper section you can right-click a partition to edit it further

Change drive letters
Use this to assign a drive letter so it won't clash with any external drives that may be connected in the future. In our example, drive P is a secondary Windows install

Drive properties
Select Properties to open the standard Windows Properties window for the highlighted drive. Here you can find tools for cleaning up files, sharing drives and de-fragmenting the current drive

Settings

You'll use it to…

Gain more disk space
View disk usage and recover lost space

Customise the mouse
Configure the mouse and trackpad to preferred settings

Set up File Explorer
Change the way it works to suit you better

Configure OneDrive
Check usage and tweak the settings of OneDrive

Use File History
Back up your files so you will never lose them

Reset the PC
Solve problems by resetting Windows to defaults

Windows 10 secrets

Top tips you need to know to enable you to work smarter and more efficiently

View disk usage

Is the disk drive becoming full, leaving very little room for files and apps? If you are not sure then check the amount of space that is used and free using File Explorer.

Recover lost space

If you have a very large disk drive with lots of free space for your photos, music, videos and apps, then you are lucky. Many people struggle for disk space and if you have an old computer that has been upgraded to Windows 10 you might find that there is little disk space left. A new PC with a solid state disk (SSD) also struggles for space because SSDs are often small. Both new and old PCs can struggle to find space for all your apps and media files. So what is the solution?

Fig 1 Right-click the disk in Explorer and select Properties to see the disk space used

Fig 2 Click Disk Clean-up in the previous screenshot and then click OK when it finishes scanning

Cleaning up the disk drive can release several gigabytes of free space and it can make a significant difference to the computer. With an extra few gigabytes you can add more photos, music, documents and apps. Windows provides the means to scan the disk for unnecessary files, junk and temporary files as well as ones that are no longer needed. Right-click a drive in Explorer and select Properties, then use the Disk Clean-up button.

Advanced mouse settings

Configure mouse settings

The mouse may not be something that you have thought about, but like all components in the computer, it can be customised and the settings can be changed. Click Start and then Settings. Click Devices and then select 'Mouse & 'touchpad' on the left. On the right is an option to set the primary mouse button to left or right. Left handed people might find it more convenient to click with the right button because it is their index finger.

1 Double-click speed Open the Control Panel and click Mouse. Set the double-click speed.

2 Pick a pointer Select the Pointers tab and choose the style from the Scheme list.

Customise the touchpad

If you use a laptop computer, it will have a touchpad or trackpad. There may be left and right buttons below it, or the touchpad itself may be used as a button for clicking. Sometimes the bottom right corner is use to right click. It is also possible to tap with one finger for a left click or two fingers for a right click. Pinch and spread, and swiping up/down or left/right with one, two or three fingers might be used to perform functions too. Go to Start>All apps and click Control Panel. Look for Trackpad, Touchpad, or something similar to access the settings. The options may vary, so choose what suits you.

3 Set pointer options Set the mouse speed on the Pointer options tab and set trails too.

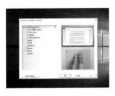

Find the trackpad settings in the Control Panel for various tap, drag and swipe actions

4 Spin the wheel Set the number of lines to scroll when spinning or tilting the mouse wheel.

Windows 10 secrets

Configure File Explorer

Many of the features of Explorer were in Windows 8, but the Windows 10 version has some new features that were not in previous versions of the app and here we take a look at them.

Explorer has a search box in the top right corner and it is useful for finding files on the disk. Click in the box, type a word to identify the file and hit Enter. Explorer scans the disk and displays the search results. Explorer is good at finding files when you know the name, but what if you aren't sure what it is called? If you know what is in the file, such as a document, you can search within files for words and phrases.

Select the View tab in Explorer, click the Options button and then Change folder and search options. Select the Search tab in

Fig 3 Select the option search for file contents to improve the search results

Quick access toolbar	Startup options	Save clicks	Privacy options
Click this button and there are six tools that can be added as icons. Tick the ones you want	There is a choice of starting Explorer with 'Quick access' or 'This PC.' Try both and pick your favourite	Normally files and folders must be double clicked, but select this to enable them to be single clicked	Frequently accessed files and folders can be displayed in the 'Quick access view' or hidden. It's your choice

Go to Settings>Devices> AutoPlay. Choose what do to with files on drives and cards.

the window that is displayed. There is an option to Always search file names and contents. Tick the box. Searches take longer, but are more thorough. If you have zip files, which are compressed archives containing one or more files, there is an option to include them in the search. Tick the box if you need to search within zips.

Configure OneDrive

OneDrive provides free online storage for your files and it is particularly useful for storing backups of files and photos, and for sharing files across two or more computers. There are some configuration options that can be used to change the way it works. Click the little up arrow at the right side of the taskbar to see a status report. It shows whether the OneDrive folder on the computer is synced with OneDrive online. Right-click the icon and a menu is displayed. Select Manage Storage to open a web browser window that shows how much space you have and how much is free. Select Settings on the menu and a small window opens with several tabs containing configuration settings. These enable you to set performance options, choose whether OneDrive starts with Windows and other options.

Manage OneDrive

1 Check OneDrive space Right-click OneDrive and select Manage storage to see your online space usage.

2 Customise OneDrive settings Right-click OneDrive and click Settings. Save files to the PC or OneDrive.

Use File History

1 Control Panel Open the Control Panel on Start>All apps, and then click File History.

2 Turn it on File History saves backups of files to an external disk for security. Click Turn on.

3 Back up files Click 'Run now' to back up files and store a copy on the external disk.

4 Set advanced settings Click Advanced Settings and choose how often to back up files.

Set privacy options

1 Location, location Some apps can work out your location. Use the switches to block them.

2 Who's watching? Use these switches to prevent unwanted apps from accessing the webcam.

3 Too familiar Cortana gets to know your voice and writing. Stop it if you prefer.

4 Friendly access Do you want apps to access your contacts? Block them if you don't.

Check app sizes by going to Settings>System> Storage. Click the disk and then apps.

Recover from faults

Problems are rare, but if you are really unlucky then a serious one might require the PC to be reset. This solves many problems and it gets the PC working again. Click Start>Settings>Update & Security> Recovery. Click 'Get started' under Reset this PC.

There are three ways to reset the PC and the first is 'Keep my files'. This removes apps and settings, and refreshes Windows with the default settings, but it keeps your files in the Documents, Pictures, Videos and Music folders. You will not lose any files, so this is a safe option to try.

The second option, 'Remove everything', completely erases everything – Windows, Settings, your files and so on. It installs a fresh copy of Windows, but you must copy your files to an external disk before starting. The third option, 'Restore factory settings', also erases everything and it puts the PC back as it was when you bought it. Back up your files first.

Increase your privacy

There are many privacy settings in Windows 10 and in fact, there are more than in previous versions of the operating system. This

Increase Wi-Fi privacy

1 Hide your computer Switch on 'Find devices and content' at home, and off in public.

2 Shared Wi-Fi Wi-fi Sense shares login details with others, but can be blocked.

gives you greater control over what can be shared and who sees information about you and your computer. The amount of information shared looks scary at first, but there is nothing to be concerned about and if you really don't want to share anything, there are controls to block everything.

An example is the Privacy options when using Wi-Fi networks. Go to Start>Settings>Network & Internet>Wi-Fi>Advanced options. Use the switch to make your PC discoverable by others or to hide it. The idea is that you can share stuff at home, but hide a laptop when using a public Wi-Fi hotspot. Go to Start>Settings>Network & Internet>Wi-Fi>Manage Wi-Fi settings. There are options to share network login details with your friends and contacts. It is your choice. Clear the tick boxes if you don't.

There's a section in Settings dedicated to privacy and we take a look at them in the following pages. There are 13 sections, you should look at each one and change any settings you don't like.

Fig 4 Choose how much diagnostic and usage data Microsoft receives. Basic is the minimum setting

Camera and microphone
The Camera and Microphone sections show what apps can access these components. Block apps that don't need access

Speech and typing
Your speech, typing and writing can be analysed to provide better search results, but can be blocked for privacy

Your ad ID
An ID code is assigned to you so advertisers can track you. It's anonymous, but you can disable it here

Website access
Websites can access information about you. This setting prevents them from knowing your language, hence your location

Fig 1 File Explorer helps you to keep organised

Fig 2 The Windows Store is where you buy apps

Fig 3 Edge is the new web browser in Windows

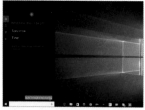
Fig 4 Cortana is there to be your assistant

Fig 5 Build great presentations in PowerPoint

Windows apps

Your quick guide to Window's 10 home apps and what you can expect from them

File Explorer File Explorer (Fig 1) enables you to browse the contents of disk drives, access files and organise them into folders. You can open files, run applications and access OneDrive content.

Control Panel Before Windows 10 introduced the Settings app there was the Control Panel. It is still there and it contains many configuration settings for Windows.

Action Centre/Notifications Notifications are designed to keep you informed about system events that require your attention, incoming email messages, and update messages from apps you use.

Windows Store A few apps are bundled with Windows 10, but there are thousands more in the Store (Fig 2) and many are free. Buy movies, TV shows and music too.

Edge Internet Explorer is still available for web browsing, but Windows 10 has a better, faster, more powerful browser called Edge (Fig 3). Use it to access the web.

Cortana Cortana (Fig 4) is a personal digital assistant. Speak to Cortana and it understands what you say and carries out actions and results of searches.

Mail Mail is an email app that can be used with accounts over at **Outlook.com**, Gmail and other email providers. It has a great interface and is touch-enabled.

Skype Whether you want to send an instant message to someone, place a voice or video call, Skype is perfect. Skype to Skype calls are free of charge.

Receive Notifications in the Action Centre with Windows 10. Find out more on page 60

48

Amalgamate your different email accounts in one place with Windows Mail app

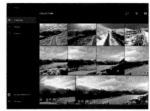

Fig 6 Organise images easily in the Photos app

 Microsoft Word Word is the word-processing application that everything else is compared to. It has more features than any rival word processor and is brilliant for home or work.

 Microsoft Excel Excel is a powerful spreadsheet application that is most commonly used for work, but students and home users will also find lots of uses for it too.

 Microsoft PowerPoint When you have a presentation to give, PowerPoint (Fig 5) is the app most people go to. Create impressive slideshows with text, images, videos and animations.

Fig 7 Access top artists with a Grove music pass

 OneDrive Microsoft provides a generous 15GB of online storage space (Fig 9). Everything is synced with a folder on the disk and files are accessed using File Explorer.

 Calendar Calendar is the place to store upcoming appointments, meetings, holidays and anything else you need to schedule. It reminds you of upcoming events.

 Camera Most computers have a camera and this app can be used to take photos and shoot videos of whatever is happening in front of the computer screen.

Fig 8 The Film & TV app stores all your videos

 Photos Transfer photos from a digital camera or mobile phone and browse them, organise them and view them with the Photos app (Fig 6). It's great for photographers.

 Groove Music Sign up for a music pass and Groove (Fig 7) can be used to play millions of tracks from top artists. It can also be used to play your own music.

Fig 9 OneDrive lets you store your files online

 Film & TV Buy or rent movies and TV shows in the Store and watch them with this app (Fig 8). It can also be used to browse and view your own videos.

 The Xbox App Keen games players will find this app useful for keeping up with their Xbox buddies (Fig 10). Keep in touch with the Xbox Live community and games.

 News The News app brings you the top news stories and headlines as they happen. It covers both local news events and stories from around the world.

Fig 10 The Xbox App is useful for gamers

File Explorer

Manage the files and folders that make up the contents of your hard drive

You'll use it to…

Browse your files
View and explore your hard drive contents

Manage your content
Move or copy files to other locations

Search your hard drive
Use the search tool bar to find files

Create new folders
Arrange your files as you see fit

Preview your files
View a preview before opening a file

Compress larger files
Save space by zipping files

Introducing File Explorer

The File Explorer plays a key part of your Windows 10 experience. The main section displays the contents of your folders while the others help you navigate your way around the contents of your PC.

Browse files and folders

The main function of File Explorer is to browse, open and manage the files stored on your hard drive (Fig 1). Across the top of the Explorer window is the ribbon; click on the Home tab to access tools such as moving, copying, renaming and deleting files. These functions can also be accessed by right-clicking on a file or folder and selecting from the menu that appears. Just below the ribbon is the address bar; this indicates the location on your hard drive that is currently being viewed within the main window. Depending on your settings you may also have a navigation pane running down the left side of the window (Fig 2). This can be used a way of quickly jumping between your libraries and favourite folders.

Fig 1 File Explorer is where you can browse and organise your files

Fig 2 You can add a navigation bar to left of the screen to help you find items

You can also use the right-hand side as a method of previewing a file without having to open it. This can show images and documents that you have created.

Manage your files

Search for files

Windows 10 includes a very useful search function that is just the thing for tracking down files. You will find it towards the top-right area of the File Explorer window. Simply start typing in the box and any matching results will appear in the main file window. The results will be matches found in the currently selected folder. If you click within the search box, an icon in the top left titled 'This PC' will appear. Use this to search every location.

File management

Your hard drive is essentially made up of files which reside within folders. Folders are a way of keeping everything organised on your hard drive. Within a folder you can have any number of files, as well as more folders – known as sub folders. When a new program is installed, you'll find that it will be placed into its own dedicated folder within your Program Files folder (also known as a directory). When arranging files yourself, you can also create your own folders and name them as you see fit.

    You can move and copy files around your hard drive to arrange them into your folders. Moving a file is known as 'cutting'; it involves taking a file from one location and placing it into another. Copying a file is similar, but the outcome is that a duplicate version of the file is created in another location while the original file remains where it was. By right-clicking a file, you can also use the 'Send To' tool to quickly move a file to another location.

1 Create folder Right-click and select New>Folder, or select New Folder from the ribbon.

2 Copy/move Left-click the file or folder you wish to manage, then select Move or Copy to.

3 Select location Click a location from the list, or Choose Location and browse for a folder.

4 Right-click method Alternatively, right-click a file and use the Cut, Copy, Paste options.

Quickly select all files within a folder by pressing Ctrl+A at the same time

Change display options

File Explorer has a variety of ways in which it can display your files and folders. It can also arrange them into orders that go beyond alphabetical sorting.

Starting with the visual aspect, your files can be shown in a list, as tiled icons or thumbnail images. These views can be chosen by clicking the View tab at the top of window, followed by clicking an entry from the selection underneath. There is also a Detail view that shows your files in a table along with detailed information (such as file size, date modified etc). When in Detail view, you can decide what details are visible by right-clicking on the column titles at the top of the display (Fig 3). You can also left-click on these column titles to reorder the currently viewed files based on the clicked

Fig 3 With the Detail option you can view and decide which columns are visible within File Explorer

Add a pane
Use these to add useful panes for navigation, previewing files or viewing file details

Navigation buttons
Use these arrows to navigate forward and backwards between folders or to go up a level

Viewing options
These options are very useful for arranging your viewed files in optimum order

Collapsible headers
These headers are used to separate groups of folders; click them to make them collapse

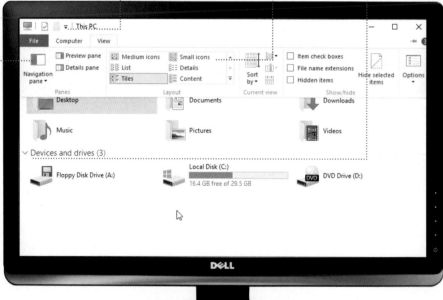

Click on Manage> Slide Show in a photo-based folder to start an instant slide show

topic. If you're not in Details view, you can still reorder the files by clicking the Sort By' button and selecting an option from the menu. Windows 10 also has a handy Group By option that can bunch together files based on a certain measurement; for example, you can batch photos together based on what day they were taken.

Virtual file libraries

Libraries are collections of certain kinds of files based on a theme. They work in a virtual manner: the files aren't literally stored in these libraries, they are merely collated and linked to the library. By default these types include pictures, music, videos and documents. Strangely they are initially hidden in Windows 10.

To make the libraries appear in File Explorer, click on View followed by Navigation Pane in the top-left corner. You can then click Show Libraries from the menu that appears; it will show a tick next to it to indicate that it is visible. You can edit an existing folder by right-clicking an existing library and select Properties. You can then add and remove folders from the selected library. Below this are options to set the library icon and to optimise the library for a specific file type.

Create a library

1 Add and rename Right-click on Library and select New>Library. You can then enter a new name.

2 Add files/folders Right-click your new library and select Properties. Use the Add button to add folders.

Create zip file

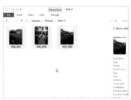

1 Select files Hold down Ctrl and click on the files you wish to add to a compressed file.

2 Send to… Right-click on your selected files. Drag your mouse pointer to highlight 'Send To'.

3 Compress files Select 'Compressed (Zip Folder)' to process your selected files.

4 Rename folder A new zip folder will be created containing your files. Rename it as required.

Control Panel

Get under the bonnet of Windows 10 via the Control Panel

You'll use it to…

Mange your devices
Install, update or disable connected devices

Control power options
Decide how and when Windows powers down

Schedule tasks
Create tasks that run at a designated time

Choose display setup
Determine how Windows 10 looks and feels

Protect your system
Create restore points to protect your setup

Select input devices
Set up voice recognition or an on-screen keyboard

Taking control

The Control Panel is where you can change the settings of Windows. The options here will affect how Windows looks and works. By taking time to learn them you can tweak your setup into working how you want it to.

Launching Control Panel

There is more than one way to launch Control Panel and also more than one way to view it. First let's look at how to open Control Panel. Using your mouse, you can move your pointer to the upper or lower corner of the right-hand side of the display. From here, drag the pointer up or down to make the Charms bar appear. Select Settings followed by Control Panel. Alternatively, drag your mouse to the bottom left of the screen and right-click on the Windows icon. You can then select Control Panel from the menu that appears.

Once the Control Panel is open, you'll see the options that are available to you. By default they are summarised by category (Fig 1).

Fig 1 The Control Panel can walk you through all kinds of tweaks and alterations

Fig 2 Here we have selected the large icon view which shows all of the options that are available

54

If you wish, you can also use the 'View By' option to adjust how the icons are visualised. You can choose to have either large (Fig 2) or small icons displayed next to the tools that are at your disposal.

Device Manager

The Device Manager is where you can view and maintain all of the internal and external devices that connect to your computer. From here you can update drivers, disable or un-install devices. Click an arrow next to a device type to view the related installed hardware. Right-click on a device to access the Device Manager menu. If a device is not installed correctly it will be highlighted with a yellow icon.

Manage Power Options

Whether you're using a laptop or desktop PC, power consumption is an important aspect to understand and set up correctly. With a desktop setup you may want your computer to sleep or shut down after a certain amount of inactivity. When using Windows on a laptop you may want it to conserve power when running purely on batteries. Such setups can be created by customising a Power Plan. Open the Control Panel and select Power Options (in the category view you will find it under Hardware and Sound). Windows will now display the current plan that is in effect. You can also select an alternative plan and Windows will apply it immediately.

Next to each option is a link titled 'Change Plan Settings'. Select this to further tweak settings such as the general screen brightness (the brighter the screen the higher the battery drain) and how long it takes for the computer to switch off the display or go to sleep when not in use.

You can always reset Power Plans back to default settings if you make unwanted changes

Create a restore point

1 Search for System Restore
Enter 'System Restore' in the Control Panel search box.

2 Initiate System Restore Select 'Create a Restore Point' from the results followed by 'Create'.

3 Name your restore point Add a title that relates to why you're creating a restore point.

4 Restore point created Now sit back as Windows creates your system restore point.

Control Panel

Using Task Scheduler

The Control Panel provides access to the Task Scheduler. With this you can create automated tasks that come into effect at a time chosen by yourself. It's a useful tool for setting up your own regular procedures. Perhaps you want to create your own regular maintenance cycle or have a daily blank word document open up as a prompt to write a new blog post.

Task Manager can be accessed by selecting 'System & Security' from the Category view in Control Panel followed by Schedule Tasks. If you're viewing Control Panel in an icon view you'll need to select Administrative Tools and then Task Scheduler. It's worth noting at this point that you will need to be logged in as an administrator on your PC.

Fig 3 Create automated tasks and personalise them as you see fit

Task Scheduler library
Click this to view your created tasks and edit them as required. They can disabled or deleted

Task status
This section contains the status of any current tasks. You can adjust the time period in the drop-down menu

Active tasks
This part shows your active tasks and their scheduled timings. Note the Open Notepad task that we have created

Creating tasks
We've covered creating basic tasks. You can also use the Create Task option to apply more conditions for your task

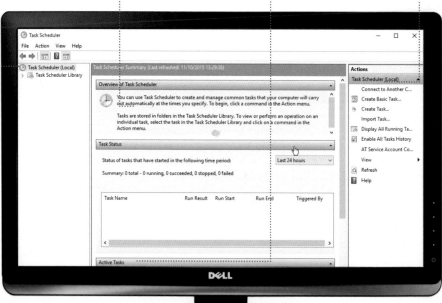

Let Windows suggest the ideal accessibility settings for you by clicking 'Get Recommendations'

With the Task Scheduler open, click on 'Create Basic Task' in the top-right section of the screen. In the next window you can enter a name and description of the task (Fig 3). After this you can set how often the task occurs. Options include time-based measurements or event-based triggers such as when you log in. You can then choose the action that occurs; it will then be added to the task list.

Ease of access

Windows includes a number of settings that help make your PC easier to use should you have difficulty with the standard setup. These can be found by opening the Ease of Access centre from within the Control Panel. Upon doing so you'll notice that your computer will be audibly explaining the contents of the screen; this is the narrator, a tool that conveys the screen content via speech, assisting users who find it difficult to view the display. Another tool that can also help visually is the magnifier. Select this and the display will enlarge along with zoom controls that allow you to manipulate the display. There is also a high contrast option which can greatly alter the colour scheme into a more readable palette. This can be toggled by pressing left Alt, left Shift and Print Screen together.

Alternative input devices

1 On-screen keyboard Select this to display a large keyboard to input text and navigate menus.

2 Speech recognition You can also use your microphone to control Windows via speech.

Set default actions

1 Open defaults Select Default Programs in the Control Panel (under 'Programs').

2 Set defaults We'll set default apps to open certain file types. Click 'Set Your Default Programs'.

3 Pick a program Select a program from the left-hand side of the display.

4 Choose types Now choose the file types that this program will open by default.

Restore your PC

1 Roll back To revert to a previous restore point, search Restore Point in Control Panel.

2 System restore Click 'Create Restore Point' from the results; 'System Restore' on next screen.

3 View previous points Click Next to see saved restore points. Select one and click Next.

4 Confirm restore Windows 10 will confirm that you wish to proceed. Click Next to do so.

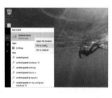

Search for Control Panel in the Start screen, then create a shortcut by right-clicking the result

Adjust system sound

At some point you'll likely need to access to the audio capabilities of your PC. From the Control Panel's category view, select 'Hardware and Sound'. On the next page, click 'Adjust System Volume'. This will open a new window that resembles a mixer. Depending on your setup you may see more than one fader. On the left is the device volume, which controls the overall volume. Other faders relate to other programs that may be running on your PC at the time. This means you can set varying levels of volume between a music-playing program, for example, and audio that may be playing in a web browser. Under every fader is a speaker icon; click it to mute the sound for that particular channel. If you mute the leftmost channel (device volume), all channels will be muted.

PC display options

There is a good deal of flexibility available when it comes to the appearance of Windows. Open the Control Panel and, in category view, select 'Appearance and Personalisation'. You'll be presented with a list of options that range from cosmetic options (wallpapers, themes etc) to more system-based ones such as screen resolutions.

Change Screen Saver

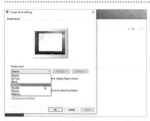

1 Pick one Click 'Change Screen Saver' from the Personalisation menu. Select a screen saver from the menu.

2 Set a time Now select how many minutes it will take for the screen saver to activate.

Control Panel

The apps

Starting at the top we have the Personalisation section. This includes options for changing your desktop background, the colour of the task bar and border, plus selecting a screen saver. Once you've set your preferences, you can save your background/screen saver/border combination as a theme. To do this, select 'Change the theme'. At the top you'll see a section titled 'My Themes'. Your current choices will be collated within the theme marked 'Unsaved Theme'. Click 'Save Theme' and enter a new name for your theme in the pop-up box. This will create a new theme in your chosen name.

Going back to the main 'Appearance and Personalisation' menu, underneath the 'Personalisation' section is a link titled 'Display'. This link contains more technical-based options that are concern tweaks such as screen brightness, colour calibration and resolution. With resolution you can make everything smaller to fit more things on the screen. Click on the adjust option and move the slider to tweak this setting (Fig 4).

Fig 4 Move the slider within the display settings screen to adjust the resolution

Windows Update
Keeping Windows updated is important to stay safe from ever evolving threats. Control the update parameters here

User Account Control
User Account Control (or UAC) prevents harmful changes from taking place. You can adjust how protective it is from here

File History
You can automatically save backup copies of your files while you work. Click File History to set this up

Add new features
You can purchase new features to add to Windows direct from Microsoft. Click on this option to see what's available

Notifications

Never miss an important event or message with notifications in Action Centre

You'll use it to...

See Mail messages
View notifications of important email messages you've received

See warning messages
Get notifications about potential Windows problems that may occur

Get tips
Read tips to help you use Windows more effectively

Read security advice
Never miss another message again about system security

Don't forget maintenance
You will be told if anything needs doing

Hear audio notifications
Hear when new notifications are in the Action Centre

Watch for notifications

Notifications keep you abreast of what is happening on your computer. By displaying pop-up messages in the corner of the screen and in the Action Centre panel you can see what's new and what needs your attention.

Open Action Centre

Notifications appear in the corner of the screen while you are using other applications for work or leisure. You might be busy and not notice them appear and they automatically disappear after a few seconds. You might see a notification and dismiss it by clicking the cross in the corner. For these reasons, notifications are collected and organised in the Action Centre and you can see recent ones listed by opening the panel on the right.

Click the Action Centre button at the right side of the taskbar. It is usually the one immediately before the clock. A panel opens on the right and the top part of it contains recent notification messages.

Fig 1 Notifications appear in the bottom-right corner of the computer screen, like this Mail message

Fig 2 View recent notification messages by opening the Action Centre panel on the right

There are some Quick Actions buttons at the bottom of the panel and to see more notifications if there are a lot of them, click Collapse above the buttons. If you want to clear out all the notifications, for example if you have read them or they are not important, click Clear all at the top of the panel.

Configure notifications

Expand notifications

Only the important parts of a notification are displayed. For example, if an email message arrives in Mail then only the Mail icon, the sender and subject appears in Action Centre or the pop-up message. Open Action Centre and click the little down arrow at the right of a notification message to read more of the text. You might not see everything, as some notifications can be too long, but shorter ones show in full.

1 Set options Go to Start> Settings>System>Notifications & actions. Turn on useful ones.

2 Set notifications Scroll to the bottom and use the switches to turn app notifications on/off.

Take action

Some notifications are merely bits of information and they might be useful, but you can ignore them. Other notifications require your attention or you may need to perform an action. If an important email arrives, for example, then click the notification pop-up in the corner of the screen or the entry in Action Centre to open the Mail app and show the message. You can then deal with the message. Another notification could be from Windows Defender, warning you that it has been some time since the computer was last scanned for malware. Click the notification and start Windows Defender, then click the button to perform a system scan.

Other notifications require different actions, so click them and see what happens. These notifications very useful and enable you to deal with anything important that arises.

3 Set the timer Click Start> Settings>Ease of access>Other options and set a time.

To set quiet hours, look to the bottom of the Action Centre screen and click 'Quiet hours'

4 Check your apps Some apps have notification preferences in their settings, like the Mail app.

Windows Store

The new Universal Windows Store is the main hub for downloading new content and managing existing apps

You'll use it to…

Download new apps
Buy/download more apps to your device

Manage existing apps
Updates to apps are handled by the Store

Grab some films
Get films from the store to watch later

Fancy some music?
Use the store to boost your music library

Redeem those codes
Use Redeem codes to unlock new content

Re-install previous content
Quickly re-install apps from My Library

Windows Store

Windows 10's Store is the main source for updating and installing new apps, downloading music or even renting the latest Hollywood blockbuster (Fig 1). It also offers a universal appeal, which means that select apps such as Word Mobile will function pretty much the same across all Windows 10 platforms.

Navigating the Store

We are pretty confident that you'll be able to navigate through the interface with ease, due to the new continuity that runs throughout. For example the tabs at the top offer quick access to new apps, the latest games, music, and films and TV. Each header pretty much looks the same when you access it, so you do not have to re-learn anything. Starting from the Home tab you can scroll down the page to view the best crop of apps and services on offer. Additionally if you hover to the sides of each section you can click and scroll

Fig 1 The Windows Store is the one stop shopping centre for all your app and multimedia needs

Fig 2 When browsing through the store extra navigation options can appear when you hover your mouse over them

horizontally through the choices or you can click on 'Show all' to see the full list of available content (Fig 2). You can also use the top left back button to quickly return to a previous screen. If you head back to the top of the Home page you can even access the 'App top charts & categories' option, which will reveal a range of categories to the left side as well as Refine options at the top. The latter are useful for fine-tuning exactly what you want the store to show.

Search for faster results

While navigating the Store is straightforward, if you are looking for a specific app or service one of the fastest ways to do this is to use the embedded search engine from the top of the store. Once this is selected you can then enter what you are looking for. Type in what you are looking for and you'll notice that the search engine will immediately start to list all the apps and services it finds. You can then select the item beneath to access the content.

Choosing what to download

Once you have found content from the store you can select the thumbnail image to gleam additional information about the item before you commit to downloading or buying it. For the most part, a brief description will be available to you at the top of the screen, which can be expanded further using the More icon. If you keep scrolling further down the page you may find screenshots alongside a Mobile or PC tab so you can switch between them to see what the app looks like in action on different platforms. Directly below this are the reviews alongside a score out of five. Finally to the side you also have recommended applications or services that other people like, which may give you an idea of what to download next.

You can use the small Account icon at the top of the page to redeem codes to use in-store

Download a free app

1 Find your item Navigate through to the store and select the free item you want.

2 Download Icon Now click the Free icon at the very top of the page.

3 Downloading your app Your app will now start to download to your device.

4 Launch your Application Now click the Open icon to launch the app or use the Start menu.

Windows Store

How to download content

Our handy tutorial has already covered the process of downloading a free app. However in order to download any items from the store, including paid for content, you will need a Microsoft account and a payment card attached for purchases. Thankfully you can quickly add a card to your account if you select the small circular Account icon, that depicts your profile picture, at the top right of the store and choose Payment Options. This will then launch Microsoft's website where you can login and add the card. When it comes to downloading or buying items you will find an icon at the top of the page and this will either show the word Free, Install (if you already own it) or it will have a currency symbol inside to showcase the cost in your native country. Additionally certain items will have a

Fig 3 When buying items you have an extra drop-out window appear to cancel the purchase

A common theme
The main interface provides a continuity that runs throughout all the tabs/ sections of the Windows Store

Featured items
The Main tabs at the top contain a large slideshow depicting the featured items within the store

Account icon
The small circular account icon (depicting your profile picture) is the place to go to manage your accounts and downloads

Search bar
If you know what you are looking for within the store you can quickly search for the item in question

Certain apps will work on both your Windows 10 Mobile and Windows 10 PC

'+' symbol included and this indicates the app will support in-app purchases. Don't worry if you are buying items directly from the store because a prompt will appear asking for your password, you can use this to confirm your purchase before committing to buy (Fig 3). Additionally most applications will offer a free trial, so you can try before you buy.

Managing your downloads

When you are apps are downloading you will briefly see a progress bar – where the Free or Paid icon appeared – with the option to pause the download, restart or use the x icon to delete. However the Store has a dedicated section for managing downloads and this is split into apps that you have previously purchased, and to managing recent downloads or updates. To access these options you need to select your small account icon at the top of the page and choose either 'My library' or 'Downloads and Updates'. The latter enables you to pause downloads again, restart them or remove them with the 'x' icon. More importantly you can also click on the 'Check for updates' icon to check for any new updates to existing apps.

Set automatic updates

1 Settings option Tap on the small Account icon at the top of a page and choose Settings.

2 Enable Automatic downloads To ensure your apps get updated toggle the app updates to on.

Install previously purchased apps

1 Main Account icon First click on the small Account icon at the top of the page.

2 My Library Now from the list of options click on 'My library' to see your apps.

3 App list Now look to the side of each app for the downward pointing icon.

4 Download the app Now select the download icon to install the app back to your device.

Microsoft Edge

Edge is the new web browser on Windows 10 and it packs in a host of features

You'll use it to...

Browse the web
Use Edge to discover content from around the world

Reading Articles
Use Reading View to read articles without any distracting Ads

Annotate your page
Draw directly on a web page to add annotations

Add Favourites
Save articles to your favourites for archiving

Add to Reading List
Save articles for reading later

Private Browsing
Browse without fear of tracking cookies

Your new browser

Microsoft Edge enables you to browse the web for new content (Fig 1), but it also incorporates some powerful new features including the ability to annotate a web page, via Web note and use a Reading View to read articles without any distracting ads or pictures.

Browse the web

By default when you launch Microsoft Edge it will display a start-page that is similar in some ways to MSN as it provides a range of news articles that you can click on to view. Thankfully you can replace the start-page, via the More Actions…>Settings option at the top right of the page, with your own website such as Google. For the most part, the top of the start page will display a 'Search or enter web address' field box, which you can select to search for items on the web or enter a direct web address such as **www. imagine-publishing.co.uk**. However what's useful here is the browser will automatically suggest addresses beneath, so you don't

Fig 1 Edge provides standard browsing options mixed in with a new Web Note tool

Fig 2 Edge will automatically provide suggestions based on your inputted URL

have to type the whole URL in (Fig 2). After the web page loads you can then use the top left icons to move forwards and backwards through pages or use the Refresh icon – which looks like a circle with an arrow through it – to reload the page.

Utilise tabs

At the top of each web page you can click on the '+' icon to add a new tab – which is essentially providing another canvas for you to search or enter a web address. What's useful is you can have multiple tabs open at once and manage these by clicking on the tab to switch between them or long pressing on a tab (with your left mouse button) and dragging it into a different position. You can also close tabs by clicking on the top right 'x' in the tabs corner.

Browse more privately

When you browse for articles the software will usually track what pages you have visited and likewise the source website may have tracking cookies of their own. These are mostly harmless as they simply report back to the author the visitors browsing habits, like how long you were on a page. Even so you may not appreciate this process, but thankfully the Edge browser can help with this by allowing you to tap into what it calls an InPrivate window. Basically you can access this option by clicking on the top right 'More actions…' icon and from here select New InPrivate Window. This will then open up a new browser window, which will enable you to search or enter websites as you did before. However this time it won't track your history or cookies. It also deletes any temporary files once the browsing session has finished.

Like the InPrivate window, you can use More Actions…>Settings to clear your browser's data

Set your default page

1 More Actions Icon Tap the 'More actions…' icon at the top and choose Settings.

2 Open with Now look for the option 'Open with' and select 'a specific page or pages'.

3 Customise! From the drop down choose Custom then click the 'x' next to the existing page.

4 Enter your new page Beneath type in your web address and click the '+' icon to add.

Read articles a little easier

While the internet is full of content (some good, some bad) the main method of reading this from a traditional browser is to view it directly on the page. The problem here is that you could be distracted from the article by adverts or possibly find it difficult to read (especially if you are short of site) if the choice of font (size or style) is not easy on the eye. Thankfully Microsoft's Edge browser has a useful tool called Reading View to help combat this problem. Basically if you browse to an article on the web, once the page loads you will notice a book icon at the top right part of the interface. If you select this it will keep the majority of the article intact, but it will remove the Adverts and any distracting side-links – to allow you to focus entirely on the source matter. Additionally you can click

Fig 3 The Reading View's font and background can be adjusted in settings

The browser window
Once your page displays it will feature in the main window. However you can navigate backwards/forwards between pages using the top arrow icons

Home icon
Missing by default the Home icon can be enabled via More actions…>Settings> Advanced settings

Enter URL's
At the top of each page there is a place where you can search for content or directly enter a website URL

Top row of icons
The remaining icons will provide access to your Reading View, Favourites and the intuitive Web Note feature

With multiple tabs open, you can now hover over opens tabs to preview the open web page

on the 'More actions…' icon at the top right corner and choose Settings (Fig 3). From here, look for the Reading section, which will allow you to adjust the background of the Reading View and more importantly the Font size. To quit out of the Reading View you just re-click the book icon at the top.

Add to Favourites and Reading list

At the top of each webpage you visit you will notice a Star icon. Clicking on this will provide you with two options, the first is to assign the page to your favourite's folder and the second is to save it to a Reading list. Technically they both do the same thing, but think of a favourite as something you want to gain access to long term, while a Reading list is something you haven't got time to read now, but will read it later (thus more disposable). With Favourites though you can choose the option 'Create new folder' and then save similar articles in the future into this folder for managing and faster retrieval later on. Alternatively choose the 'Create in' drop down list and save to your Favourites bar, see the tutorial below. In order to retrieve the Favourite or Reading list article after it's saved you can click on the Hub icon at the top of the interface.

Add a Favourites bar

1 Head to Settings First click on the 'More actions…' icon at the top and choose Settings.

2 Enable Favourites bar From Settings toggle the Favourites bar to on. You can now access favourites.

Third party favourites

1 Access the Hub From the top of the browser select the Hub icon.

2 Import Favourites Now select the Favourites icon and then click on 'Import favourites'.

3 Choose Browser Next choose your browser from the list and click Import.

4 Access imported favourites In Favourites choose the Favourites bar folder to access them.

Tap into Cortana

1 Advanced Settings Select More actions…>Settings>View Advanced Settings.

2 Enable Cortana Support Toggle on 'Get Cortana to assist me' in Microsoft Edge.

3 Find Article text Head back to the main browser window and locate an article with text.

4 Ask Cortana Using the mouse highlight a word within the article and choose Ask Cortana.

Using the Hub Icon you can also access your web History and downloads you've made.

Additional options and settings

We have already touched base on a few of the settings options already, but the main focal point is to use the 'More actions…' icon at the top of the interface. Foremost this will allow basic functions such as Print or Find. The latter allows you to search for words on the current page. Additionally you can open the page in Microsoft Edge, which may be useful for developers wishing to see what their site is like in the original browser. However the Settings>Advanced settings option is likewise useful. If you drill down to Advanced settings you can add extra security to your browser via a Pop-up blocker to stop websites from launching ads in separate windows or adjust how cookies are handled (there are various other privacy settings to be gleamed also). Additionally you can enable Cortana support, which we showcase in a separate tutorial. It's worth investigating the 'More actions…' icon and its many sub-options, to get the most from the browser.

Make a Web Note

One of the most exciting features of Edge is the ability to create Web Notes and save them locally or share with others; thus instead

Share a Web Note

1 Share Option After creating your Web Note choose the top right Share icon.

2 Choose where to Share Now choose which app you want to share to and follow the instructions.

of sending a colleague a standard web link to an article you can send them a visual alternative instead! Basically when you access the dedicated Web Note icon at the top of the interface it actually freezes what you were looking at and from here you can annotate the page using a mouse or finger and a series of tools (Fig 4). The Tools are accessible from the top left part of the screen and you can click on the first tool to choose a Pen and colour combination before dragging a line from one point to say a specific header of an article to showcase its importance.

Likewise you can use a highlighter tool to highlight a specific sentence or paragraph on a page or add text notes via the Typed Note tool icon. Don't worry if you make mistakes though as the Eraser tool icon is there to help. Once the Web Note is finished you can either save this locally to your OneNote app or your Reading list that we spoke of before. Additionally you can share the Web Note with others.

Fig 4 A Web Note offers a means to annotate a web page using a series of intuitive tools

The Pen tool
The Pen tool provides a range of colours and sizes in which you can use to pin point areas of interest on the page

Highlighter Pen
Similar the Highlighter Pen can be used with a series of different colour options to highlight specific sentences/paragraphs of an article

Clip tool
You can use the Clip tool (scissor icon) to select/copy an area of a page and then paste the contents into a third party app

Saving
Once the Web Note is finished you can save it locally to your Favourites or Reading list

Cortana

Cortana is a virtual digital assistant that can be called upon to aid you in certain tasks

You'll use it to…

Get answers to questions
Using voice recognition you can verbally ask Cortana questions

Create emails or events
Use Cortana to create emails or add events to your Calendar

Play music
Cortana can be asked to play your favourite music track(s)

Location awareness
Cortana can tap into your location services for traffic or directional help

Set Reminders
You can add reminders with Cortana and get Notification alerts

Application support
Cortana can be used to open certain apps and services on your device

Cortana your digital assistant

Cortana is a virtual digital assistant that is integrated within the core operating system and default apps. It can be used for a number of tasks, ranging from adding events to your calendar to asking it questions such as "Who is the Queen of England?" (Fig 1).

Personalise Cortana

Next to the Windows Start Menu you'll find a search bar and this is where you can unlock Cortana. Ideally you will want to have a microphone attached to your device, as Cortana can then respond to commands using "Hey Cortana" as your opening phrase. However the first point of call is to select the Search bar and choose the Settings cog icon. From here toggle Cortana to on and when prompted input your name, Brett for instance. Once this is done select Next to finish. Now select the Search bar again and choose the Notebook icon and click on Settings. Now toggle the 'Hey Cortana' option to On. At this point you will need to run through

Fig 1 Speaking "Hey Cortana" will enable you to use your voice to directly ask Cortana various questions

Fig 2 You need to setup your Microphone to take full advantage of Cortana

a Microphone Setup process which involves speaking presets sentences (Fig 2). It's worth doing to enhance the responsiveness of Cortana. Once complete you can say "Hey Cortana" to ask it for help.

Checking your microphone level

Teach your voice

By default Cortana is set to recognise any voice, but you can train it to recognise your own voice for more accuracy. It works similar to the initial Microphone setup we spoke of earlier, but essentially you need to select the Search bar and head to the Notebook>Settings option. From here scroll down to where it says 'Learn my voice' and click on this option. You then need to speak several preset sentences to train Cortana to recognise your voice. It also gives you a heads up as to what questions you can ask Cortana.

Configure your Notebook Cards

Once Cortana is configured, overtime the Home section will start to fill up with Weather, News and Calendar events. Similar to Google Now, Cortana starts to learn your habits and you can tailor this to a certain degree by utilising the Notebook icon. From here a list of options will appear, such as 'Meetings & Reminders'. Clicking on these option headers will allow you to tailor how Cortana utilises the information it collects or how it presents the cards in the Home view. If you click on News you can scroll to the base and choose what topics and categories you want Cortana to track. Likewise click on Weather and you can set multiple cities that you want Cortana to display. Cards, such as 'Getting around' (location based), are more suitable for the Windows Phone side of things due to its location awareness and portability, but you can still ask Cortana for Traffic info for any location before you set off – which is useful.

1 Access the Control Panel In the Search bar type in 'Control panel' and click the best match.

2 Hardware & Sound From the resulting screen click on the 'Hardware and Sound' header.

3 Select your sound Next click on the header Sound and the choose the Recording tab.

4 Adjust levels Select the microphone and boost the pick up volume in Properties>Levels.

If you are feeling low you can ask Cortana to tell you a joke "Hey Cortana… Tell me a joke"

Cortana

What you can do with Cortana

A good starting point with knowing what to ask Cortana is to click the search bar and head to the Notebook option to enable 'Cortana Tips'. This will provide occasional pop-ups of what it can do. However for the most part you use the "Hey Cortana" phrase, followed by a command. Here are a few examples of the commands you can use: "Hey Cortana… Add event." Cortana will then ask you for the date and time that you want to use for the event; followed by more questions, such as what you want to call it (Fig 3). Similarly you could ask it to compose an email "Hey Cortana… Compose email." The trick is to leave a small pause after the Cortana phrase to give the system time to recognise your voice. Later you can start to string more sentences together such

Fig 3 More complex requests, such as adding an event, will prompt Cortana to ask a series of questions

Meet & Greet
When you launch Cortana, when clicking on the search bar, it will usually greet you

Home Cards
The main Home screen will usually display a series of Cards, such as Weather and News

Notebook Configuration
Using the Notebook icon you can configure how the cards on the Home screen will display

Microphone icon
As well as using "Hey Cortana" to get a response you can also click the microphone icon at the base

You can also press and hold the Win+C key together to bring up Cortana

as "Compose email to Lucy James". Don't worry if Cortana times out, you can manually click the Microphone icon in the Search bar to bring up the voice recognition again. Additional items you can say are "Hey Cortana… What's the weather like?", "What's on at the cinema," "Open Xbox app," "what's the traffic like?", "Play Brandon Flowers Crossfire" or even "243 times 23" Just keep experimenting.

Add Reminders

In Windows 10 you can set reminders based on time, place or person, they'll also sync across to your other Windows 10 devices. A time based reminder is obviously related to timed events, such as "Hey Cortana… Remind me to renew the car tax in two days at 8am." Or a Place reminder is associated with location and this could be "Remind me to buy food when I leave home." People based Reminders are also powerful, you could to set a reminder to "Speak with Lucy when I get to the office." When it detects the contact has been emailed or an email has been received it will flag up an alert. The latter alert will also flag up if a person calls your Windows 10 phone. Alerts will appear at the bottom right corner of the desktop, you can then action these by Snoozing or Completing them.

Set a Reminder

1 Hey Cortana Say "Hey Cortana… Remind me to wash the car today at 5pm." When prompted answer "yes."

2 Managing Reminders Click the Search bar and choose the 'Light bulb' icon, then select the Reminder.

Adding an Event

1 Add the Event First speak "Hey Cortana Add an event" and wait for the prompt.

2 Input Day & Time Now say the day you want to add the event and follow this by the time.

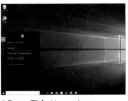

3 Enter Title Next, when prompted speak what you want the event to be called.

4 Confirm the Event A confirmation screen will now appear, so say "yes" to confirm.

People

The Universal People's app is essentially where all your contacts and the related info is held

You'll use it to…

Create contacts
You can add contacts to a chosen account

Edit existing contacts
Update existing contacts with new info and profile image

Import contacts
You can also import contacts from other accounts ie. Google

Keep track of people
Use the app to view contact details and additional info

Link contacts
You can link multiple contacts so all the info is in one place

Tap into other apps
Add an address and you can view this in the Maps app

The People app

The People app allows you to create and manage existing contacts (Fig 1). A contact could include an email address, phone number and place of work. However you can also import contacts from third party apps and services such as iCloud, Google or Exchange.

Creating or Editing Contacts

The People's app is linked to the Mail and Calendar apps, so you may find a list of contacts are already displayed. Thankfully you can easily edit, remove or create your own contacts. First creating a contact involves using the large '+' icon at the top-left part of the interface or you can edit or delete an existing contact by either right clicking on a contact or using the Pencil icon via the top-right. Whichever option you choose the resulting interface is the same (Fig 2). From here you can select Add Photo to attach a profile image from your Photo's app or you can click in the field boxes to add your contact's name, address and phone number. You can

Fig 1 If you have the Mail or Calendar app setup on your device it will automatically import contacts

Fig 2 You can use the primary interface to add detailed info about a contact

also use the '+' or drop down icons next to a field box to change the default behaviour. Thus if you add a Phone number you can choose what type, Work or Mobile. It's also worth adding an address because this will allow you to view the location on your Maps app or use the Other tab to add things like websites and birthdays. Just click the Save icon at the top right to finish.

Manipulating Contacts

If your contacts list starts to grow you can still find people quickly if you select the larger letter above the contacts name (sorted by first name by default). This will then allow you to jump to any other letter by simply clicking on it. Alternatively you can use the Search field box at the top and directly type in the contact name.

Importing from other apps

While the Microsoft account takes precedence, if you already have contacts setup in other applications, such as Google or iCloud you can import these into the app as well. The first port of call is to click on the 'More actions…' icon at the top-left of the page and then choose Settings. From here a list of options will appear and you need to select 'Add an account'. Follow this up by selecting which account you want to add like iCloud and then input your relevant security details to add the account to the People's app. Once the contacts are added you can then use the editing techniques we spoke of earlier to adjust them to taste. A useful tip is that when the account is merged you can use the 'Showing all' option from the front page to adjust what account you want to view.

If the contact has address info you can select this to view the details on the Maps app

Linking contacts

1 Select contact
From the app select the contact that you want to link.

2 Link icon
Now click on the link icon and choose Select a contact to link.

3 Search or select contact
Next you can search or select the contact you want to link.

4 Link the contact
Now you can use the back button to view the contact.

Mail

Sync multiple email accounts in one place with the Mail app

You'll use it to…

Manage all your accounts
Create multiple email accounts all within the Mail app

Sync your contacts
Access contact information from the People app

Keep a tidy inbox
Mark spam, favourite emails and flag important messages

Format your emails
Change font and colour and add lists

Create folders
Build folders to segregate your emails into

Make a custom signature
Add a personalised message to appear at the bottom of all your emails

Sending emails

The Microsoft account you use to log into Windows syncs automatically with the Mail app. Any emails you have already had sent to that account will automatically be added to the Mail app for you to start sending and receiving emails from (Fig 1).

Composing emails

The Mail app syncs itself with all of your contacts from your email account and the People app so you can quickly send emails via the app. As such, when you start composing a new email and typing in the names of the recipients, if they are stored in your People app then the emaili l addresses will instantly appear for selection as you start typing (Fig 2). To start composing a new email, click on the '+' (new mail) icon in the left-hand column and then enter the recipient(s) into the 'To' field. You can also add a subject and then add additional recipients by clicking on the 'Cc' and 'Bcc' links to the right. The main window is reserved for your email body text, so type

Fig 1 Click on the respond icon next to the New Email icon to reply to a selected email

Fig 2 (Right) By setting up a favourite contacts list, you'll save time when browsing for specific emails

in here and then use the formatting bar at the top of the screen to adjust the style of the font and paragraphs. If you wish to add attachments then click on the 'Insert' tab and pick an option.

Email settings

In the Mail app, click on the cog icon in the lower-left corner to access your settings. Click on Accounts and select a setup account to view available options. Here you can decide how far back emails that sync with the app go. Click Options in the settings menu to adjust default font and colour for all message text and also change your account's signature, which will be added to the bottom of all outgoing emails.

Formatting your emails

Once you've written out an email, you can format the text to your liking. To display the formatting tool bar, select a body of text within your email. Click the Font icon in the bottom tool bar to change your font type and size. You can also change the font colour and add a highlighting colour to selected fonts from the tool bar. In the second category of tools from the lower tool bar, the Mail app provides you with the same bold, italic and underlining tools you'd find in a word-processing program. Simply select the text you want to format and add the appropriate formatting tool. The third category of tools in the lower tool bar provides advanced formatting options. Here you can add bulleted and numbered lists to your text and insert emoticons. With a body of text selected, click on the link icon to add a hyper link to your email; insert the web address you'd like the selected text to link to, then click 'Insert link'.

From the formatting toolbar, click Options to access a handy spell-checker for your email

Add a new account

1 Account settings In the left-hand column, click on Accounts to reveal your active accounts.

2 Add an account Click on 'Add account' and then select the relevant email provider.

3 Account sign-in You will be prompted to sign into your email account.

4 Your account You can access your accounts in the column to the left of the screen.

Tidy your inbox

Once you have synced your email account with the Mail app, you can utilise the tidying tools available to help de-clutter your inbox. If you have a large number of emails that you want removed from your inbox but they are spread out throughout it, try using the search tool – it can be found at the top of your inbox. Click on the search icon, then type in the recipient's name or a search term to isolate a selection of emails. From these, select all of the emails that you want removed from your inbox. Once you have made your choice, click the bin icon in the bottom-right corner of the app. Once the emails have been removed from your inbox, they can still be found within the bin folder. So open the latter to access all of your deleted emails. You can also select emails within the bin folder

Fig 3 Emails are not permanently deleted until they're removed from the bin folder

Switch accounts
Once you've set up multiple email accounts, you can click here to switch between them

Your inbox
Emails from a particular inbox will be displayed in a list here. To select emails, click the list icon at the top of the column

Quick tools
With an email open you will see tools at the top of the screen to replay, forward, archive, delete and flag

Other options
Here you will see options to switch to Calendar, access the Feedback service and go to the Mail settings screen

To select emails in your inbox, click on the tick-list icon in the top-right corner of the app

and click the bin icon again, this time completely erasing them and making them irretrievable (Fig 3). Another way to tidy your inbox is to mark unwanted emails as junk, sending them to the Junk folder and instructing Mail to automatically do the same for any similar emails.

Organise your mail

There are several organisational tools available in the Mail app. To start with, open your Mail app settings. Click on Options and then you will be able to activate Swipe actions and then determine what those actions are. For example, for can set the swipe right/hover command to mark your emails as read/unread and the swipe left/hover command to something else, such as archive. Just click on the drop down menu to select a function from the list. You can also set up other features such as the option to show email messages by conversation (to keep things neatly organised) and to enable notifications so that you always know when an important email has arrived. You will also find a section called 'Reading' in settings where you can determine what happens to your emails once you have read them.

Pin folders

1 Select a folder Open the folder that you want to pin to your Windows Start screen.

2 Pin the folder Right-click on the folder and then select the 'Pin to Start' option.

Personalise your mail

1 Go to Settings Click on the small cog icon in the lower-left corner of the screen.

2 Click Personalisation Now, from the list of options, select 'Personalisation' from the list.

3 Choose colours Use the colour picker to choose a colour scheme for your Mail app.

4 Pick a theme You can also choose a theme that adorns the background of your menu.

Skype

Call friends and family and instant message people with the Skype app

You'll use it to…

Call people for free
Skype call, video chat and message people

Make cheap calls
Call any number across the planet for pennies

Manage your contacts
Access all of your contacts' details via Skype

IM and text messaging
Instant-message Skype users and phone numbers

Share files
Send attachments to people while you talk with them

Create a group
Add multiple participants to one conversation or video chat

Launch Skype

The Skype app can be downloaded from the Windows Store. Once it's launched, you'll need to sign in to a pre-created Skype account (Fig 1). You can't register an account through the app; you'll have to visit **skype.com** to do this. Sign in to launch the app.

Add a contact

In the home screen of the Skype app, click on the search icon. Type a name, user account, email address or phone number into the search box. Click on the search icon. If you are searching for someone who is not yet in your contacts list, click Search Skype. Skype will search for all users relevant to your search term (Fig 2). The more specific the search term, the fewer results you'll get. Searching for an email address or username will make a contact easier to find. Once you've found a contact, click on their name and 'Add to contacts'. Type a message to send along with your contact request, then click Send. Once the contact has accepted your

Fig 1 You can only have one Skype account per Windows login

Fig 2 You can also send files to or call contacts that you have not yet added

request they'll appear in your contact list. You can also save phone numbers to Skype. Right-click the click Save Number in the bottom-right corner of the app. Input a number and a country code, then click Save. The number will be added to your contacts list.

Top up credit

To add credit to your account, click on your profile image in the top-right corner. In the sidebar, click Account. You will be prompted to open the Internet Explorer app, which will take you to **skype.com**. Sign in to your account to see your current credit balance. Click Add Skype Credit. Select an amount out of the available choices, then click Continue. Select and input a payment method, then click Pay Now.

Messaging and calling

Click on a contact's name within the Skype app to display an IM window and their Skype information. Below their photo, click the Call button to make a call. If the user has provided a phone number, you can either call them on that or call their Skype account. You will need credit to call a phone via Skype. Next to the phone icon, click the '+' icon to send files to the user or to add another participant to your conversation. By adding a participant you will be taken to your contact list, where you can select someone to include. When sending a file to a user, you can browse through your files and folders via the Skype app to select the file you want to upload. Sent files will be displayed in the IM window next to the profile information. Click on the text box in the IM window to send a message to the user. Click Send Via to send the message to their Skype account or to their phone.

Right-click a contact and then click View Profile to view their details in the People app

Making video calls

1 Video calling Click on a contact, then click the camera icon below their name.

2 Calling options During a call, click on the '+' icon for more calling options.

3 Dialling pad Click on the 'dial pad' option if touch tone is needed for a call.

4 Video and audio Click on the camera or mic icon to hide your video or mute your audio.

Microsoft Word

Use Word to create letters, reports, essays and even write books

You'll use it to…

Create new documents
Create documents by selecting an attractive template

Format the text
Change the text style, font, colour and more

Insert an image
Learn how to insert images into a document

Apply image effects
Enhance images and wrap body text around them

Format paragraphs
Explore the many paragraph formatting options

Insert a table
Format text by creating and using tables

Create a document

Starting a new document is easy. Click File at the top and select New on the left. To start with a clean page, click the Blank document thumbnail (Fig 1). Now just start typing your letter, report, CV, book or whatever you want.

Choose a template

Although you can create any type of document starting with a blank sheet, you can save time and effort by using a template. Select File>New and a few templates are displayed as thumbnails, but there are many more online. Enter a word or phrase into the search box at the top, such as 'newsletter' and lots of great template thumbnails are shown; click one to see a larger version (Fig 2) and click Create if you want to use it. A template contains text and sometimes images too. These are just to show you where elements on the page are placed. Click the heading and replace it with your own, click the body text and type in your own words,

Fig 1 Select the Blank document template when you need simple or basic documents like letters

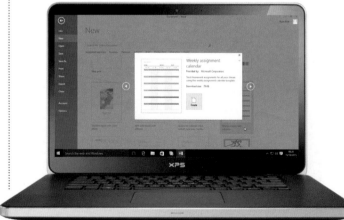

Fig 2 You don't need to be an expert to create great documents; just select a template

replace the photos with ones you have taken, delete items on the page that you do not need, and so on. Templates are so good that many people rarely use anything else and there a large number are available to suit a wide range of publications. Just search for them.

Format with styles

Word provides many shortcuts to creating great documents and one of these is styles. Click the Home tab (if it is not currently visible) and in the Style section you can click on Normal, Heading 1, Title and other styles to format the text. Whatever text is selected is formatted with the font, colour, size, line spacing and other attributes that are defined in the style. It saves you having to manually format text.

Expand the styles

Only a few styles are initially shown in the ribbon. To view them all, click the Home tab, then the bottom arrow at the right side of the styles. When a template is selected for a document, it contains its own collection of styles. This is so that no matter where in the document you create a heading, it always has the same font, size, colour and so on. Different templates use different styles.

Using the formatting tools in the Home tab of the ribbon. As shown in the step-by-step guide, you can modify a style and change the font, size, colour and so on. Expand the styles palette and down at the bottom you'll find 'Create a style'. This enables you to save the modified style under a new name. You can then select this custom style in the palette whenever you need to apply it in the document. It saves time and effort and ensures that your document always uses the same styles.

To display styles in a handy window, simultaneously press Shift+Ctrl+Alt+S

Format text

1 Select text Click and drag over text and the format tool bar appears. Click a button.

2 Choose a font Some of the items have drop-down menus, such as font selection.

3 Use special effects Select the Home tab in the ribbon to find interesting special effects.

4 Open the window Click the bottom-right button of the Font section for more features.

Insert a table

Tables are a useful way to present certain types of information and they enable you to enter text and numbers into rows and columns. Examples include names and telephone numbers, products and prices, to-do lists with dates and completion status, and so on.

The rows and columns of a table enable you to position text and numbers on the page, too. So you could create an invoice, for example, and have products and services on the left and prices on the right. All the prices in the right column would line up under one another, which would be difficult using any other method, such as by adding spaces on a line.

To insert a table into a document, first move the cursor to the place you want it. Go to the Insert tab of the ribbon and click the

Fig 3 Drag the mouse over the boxes in the ribbon to select the table size

Show or hide
Right-click the tab title and there is an option to Collapse the ribbon. This hides or shows it

Show the menu
Some items have a small arrow next to them. Click it and a menu or palette of options appears

Open windows
To save hunting for features, many sections in the ribbon can be opened in a window. Click here

Expand the window
Can't find a feature on the ribbon? It may be hidden. Make the Word window bigger to see more tools

If you need to change the header for your document, right-click it and select Edit Header

arrow under Table. There is a grid of boxes and as the mouse is moved over them, the table appears in the document. Click the mouse when the table is the size you need (Fig 3). Click in a table cell and enter the text, then tab to the next cell. Pressing Tab in the last cell adds a new row to the table.

Headers and footers

With some documents, you might want to display certain information at the top and/or bottom of each page. A simple example of this is to put a page number at the foot of each page, or the title of the document at the top. Without page numbers, you would not know which order the pages were in.

Headers and footers are inserted in the same way and both are found on the Insert ribbon tab. Click either Header or Footer as required and select from one of the options that are listed. The header/footer is added to the page and you can then edit it – for example, by entering your own text, or moving and positioning elements. When you have finished editing the header/footer, click Close Header and Footer at the right side of the ribbon bar to return to document editing.

Create a header

1 Choose a header Select the Insert tab, click Header and then click the one you want.

2 Edit the header This is a simple title header. Click in the placeholder text and enter your own.

Paragraph options

1 Align the text Use the four buttons in the Paragraph part of the ribbon to align the text.

2 Set the spacing Change the line spacing to make the text more or less dense.

3 Use indents A paragraph can be indented to make it stand out. It's useful for quotes.

4 Border & colour Add a border to a paragraph to highlight it, or set the background colour.

Alter template images

1 Change the picture Right-click an image in the template and then select Change Picture.

2 Select the source Files can be inserted from the disk, but there is clip art available too.

3 Select an image Search for an image in the clip art, select it and then click Insert.

4 Apply a style Right-click the image, click Style and select one of the special effects.

Right-click images, select Wrap Text and then choose one of the options available

Add images

Word is more than a simple word processor; it can handle images too. This makes it useful for a wide range of projects, such as newsletters, posters, cards and brochures. Some of the templates contain images; these are placeholders to show where they appear on the page. The idea is that you replace them with your own. The tutorial shows how this is achieved and it is a very easy task.

If you are creating your own document or if you want to add more images to a template, there is an Illustrations section on the Insert tab of the ribbon bar. The Pictures button is used to select a photo or image file that is on the disk drive, and the Online Pictures button enables you to search Microsoft Office clip art, Bing or your pictures in OneDrive.

Enhance images

Word has some powerful features that enable you to format and enhance images that are in the text of documents. Normally you would need to use a separate photo editor to perform the sorts of tasks that Word can do on the page. An example of this is resizing and rotating images.

Add image effects

1 Re-size and rotate Grab the handles around the edge of the image to re-size it and rotate it.

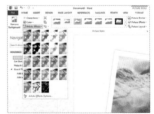

2 Get creative The Artistic Effects palette contains lots of useful special effects for images.

After using the Picture button on the Insert tab in the ribbon, the image appears on the page. At each corner is a small box – a handle – and clicking and dragging them makes the image bigger or smaller. At the top centre of the image is a round arrow and clicking and dragging this left or right rotates the image and it enables them to be placed at an angle on the page.

Double-click an image in the document and the Picture Tools on the Format ribbon tab are displayed. There are lots of functions and in the Styles section you'll find Picture Border, Picture Effects and Picture Layout. The Picture Effects are excellent and include bevel, glow, reflection, soft edges and many more effects. Within each of these are numerous variations.

In the Adjust section you can correct the brightness and contrast, apply colour filters to the image, or use special effects such as photocopy, light screen, chalk sketch, paint strokes and so on. Images can be cropped to shapes, too (Fig 4).

Fig 4 Click the Crop icon and a rectangular photo can be turned into any shape

Spelling and grammar
Have you made any typing slips or mistakes in the text? Click this button and check the spelling and grammar

Help with words
This icon accesses a thesaurus to show alternative words; above is the dictionary button to show word definitions

Translate the text
Word is able to translate the document into another language if needed. Click the button and follow the prompts

Grammar suggestions
After clicking the Spelling & Grammar button, this panel opens at the right to suggest improvements to the text

Microsoft Excel

Create spreadsheets to analyse your spending, monthly budgets and other numeric data

You'll use it to…

Create a workbook
Browse the templates and open them for editing.

Format cells
Apply fonts and sizes, colours and borders.

Enter cell data
Enter text and numeric data into spreadsheet cells.

Use functions
Use AutoSum and build your own functions.

Insert charts
Turn numeric data into easy-to-read charts.

Protect workbooks
Add password protection and other security features.

Plan and analyse

Excel is a spreadsheet app that enables you to analyse numeric data, forecast what may happen when it changes and so plan ahead. It is often used to analyse finances, but this is far from its only use.

Use a template

Spreadsheets are used by companies to analyse data relating to their business, but they are also useful for home users – for example, to monitor and analyse your monthly spending and create budgets. An Excel file is called a workbook and it contains one or more worksheets, so you could track your spending for each year in separate sheets and save them all in one workbook.

To start from scratch, click File>New>Blank workbook (Fig 1). It contains one spreadsheet and the '+' button at the bottom of the window enables extra sheets to be added in tabs. There are hundreds of ready-made workbooks and you can save a lot of time and effort by loading one that is similar to what you need and then

Fig 1 Click File>New then 'Blank workbook' to create an empty spreadsheet

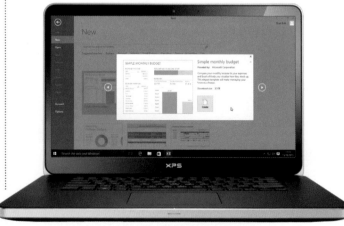

Fig 2 Save time and effort by using the spreadsheet templates. Many of them are really useful

customising it. Click File>New and enter a word or phrase to search for, such as budget, invoice, calendar or expense (Fig 2). Matching workbooks are shown as thumbnails and clicking one shows a larger image and file details. Click Create to open the workbook.

Advanced formatting

Enter data

Click any cell in the sheet and you can enter text or numbers. Excel can usually tell what has been entered, but to avoid confusion, use the correct cell format option. This is needed for telephone numbers, otherwise Excel strips off leading zeros. Numbers are right-aligned and text is left-aligned, but the Alignment section of the Home tab has buttons to left, centre or right align the contents of a cell.

1 **Set currency** Many templates use dollars. Select the cells and set it to pounds via Accounting.

Format cells

On the Home tab of the ribbon are lots of controls for formatting cells and in the Font section you can select the font and the size of the cell contents. It has no effect on the calculations performed, but it can help to make a spreadsheet containing lots of numbers and text easier to read. Choose a large font for the title and make it bold by clicking the B icon. Click the paint bucket icon or the arrow next to it to select a background colour; click the font colour icon and so on. Colour the headings placed in columns or rows and highlight important cells, such as totals or the result of calculations. This draws the eye towards them.

The spreadsheet grid shows where the cells are, but it often helps to draw a heavier line around certain cells to highlight or separate them. Click the arrow next to the border icon in the Font section of the Home tab to display a list of borders you can apply.

2 **Apply styles** Click and drag over some cells, then choose a cell style in the ribbon.

3 **Format tables** Select some cells, click Format As Table and select one of the styles.

Click the top-left corner of the spreadsheet in order to apply formatting to all cells

4 **Hide pennies** Use the buttons in the Number tab to alter the number of decimal places.

Customise the status

You can create formulas and enter them into cells to analyse the data and show various interesting facts about it, but it is not the only way to use Excel and it is possible to discover a lot of facts and figures simply by pointing and clicking within the cells. Right-click the status bar that runs along the bottom of the window and a large menu is displayed (Fig 3). The important functions are in the bottom half of this menu and you should tick Average, Count, Numerical Count, Minimum, Maximum and Sum.

Once you have done this, click in the spreadsheet to select a cell and drag down a column of numbers or money, or drag along a row of numeric data. The status bar now shows all those functions that you enabled. For example, you can see the sum of the

Fig 3 Choose what information to show at the bottom of the Excel window

Sheet tabs
Switch sheets by clicking the tabs; right-click them to delete or rename them, or set their colour

Formula bar
Click a cell to select it and then click in the formula bar to enter text, numbers or a formula

Ribbon tabs
Explore the ribbon tabs. On the View tab, for example, you can hide the spreadsheet grid lines

Extra features
Some sections of the ribbon have a tiny button in the corner. Click it to access more functions

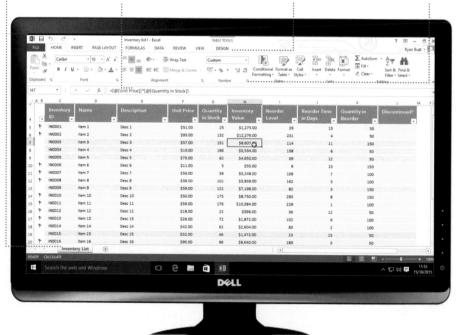

To insert or delete a row or column, right-click the column or row label to bring up a menu

numbers or money, the average value, the maximum and minimum values and so on. This feature enables you to quickly analyse part or all of the spreadsheet without even writing a single function. Just point, click and drag over cells.

Another useful interface feature is the zoom slider in the bottom-right corner. Drag the control to zoom in or out.

Use AutoSum

One of the most common uses for Excel is to find the sum of a column of numbers and this achieved with AutoSum. Click below the last cell in a column of numbers or money and click the sum button (E) in the Editing section of the Home tab. Excel enters the formula needed to calculate the total, such as **=SUM(B1:B8)**. Press Enter to accept it. Click the arrow next to the AutoSum button to insert other functions like maximum, minimum, average etc. More complex functions are entered by selecting them on the Formulas tab and entering cell references like A1, B3 and so on. Often it is sufficient to point and click on the cells to use in a formula and enter plus, minus, multiply or divide symbols between them – such as **=B2+C4**, which adds cells B2 and C4.

Use AutoSum functions

1 Find the total Click below a column of numbers and click AutoSum to insert the formula.

2 Find the maximum Click below another column, click the AutoSum arrow and select Max this time.

Use functions

1 Select a function Select a cell and then select a function on the Formulas tab, such as SUM.

2 Select the cells The SUM function requires numbers. Click and drag over the cells to sum.

3 DIY functions Click in a cell and enter = to indicate that you are building a formula.

4 Build the formula Create the formula by clicking cells and inserting plus, minus and so on.

Add a chart

1 Select the data Click and drag over the cells and titles that you want to chart.

2 Choose a chart Select the Insert tab and click the arrow next to a chart type. Pick one.

3 Move and re-size Drag the chart to position it and drag the handles to change the size.

4 Edit the chart Some chart elements, such as the title, can be changed by clicking them.

Conditional formatting can be used to highlight cells containing numbers that are less than zero

Backstage view

Excel has a Backstage view that is accessed by clicking File>Info. It displays information about the workbook and it enables you to modify settings. For example, on the right is Properties and you can give the workbook a title by clicking 'Add a title'. Tags and categories can be set and these could be used to organise workbooks or to search for them using Explorer.

The Versions section is useful and if you make a mess of a spreadsheet, you can return to a previous version of the file and undo any recent changes. Excel automatically saves a workbook as a new version every so often and these are all listed. The Protect Workbook button displays useful functions that enable you to lock a finished workbook so that it cannot be changed, such as by other people who use it. You can also encrypt the file and add a password to prevent other people from opening it.

Insert a chart

A spreadsheet full of numbers is difficult to understand and it is often hard to see what all the figures mean in simple terms. Although certain parts like totals and balances can be highlighted

Change a chart

1 Show the menu Right-click a chart and there are useful options, such as Change Chart Type.

2 Select a chart Browse the different chart types and select the one you want to use.

with coloured backgrounds, it isn't easy to see what part all the other numbers play. A simple example is your monthly bills, which are easily added to a spreadsheet to track your spending. A function will tell you the total amount, but breaking down the figures and seeing where your money is going isn't easy. A chart can make a huge difference and you can see at a glance which bills are the highest, and the proportion each bill contributes to the total.

Excel is able to create charts from financial figures or any type of numeric data and there is a wide range to choose from (Fig 4). There are the familiar pie and bar charts, but also specialised ones such as radar, doughnut, scatter and others. A great feature of Excel is that it can suggest the type of chart that is best for the data in your spreadsheet and then with a couple of clicks of the mouse, it can create it and insert it for you. There is very little work involved and often the resulting chart just needs to be dragged into position and re-sized.

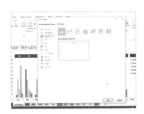

Fig 4 Select the Design tab in the ribbon and choose a style for the chart

Add illustrations
Click Illustrations in the Insert tab to add photos, shapes, online art and SmartArt – clever widgets

See recommendations
After selecting some cells, click here to see which types of chart Excel recommends that you use

Get chart info
Mouse over a chart to see info about the data. Right-click it to change the way it is displayed

Add text
You can add text boxes, such as explanatory notes, set page headers and footers and more

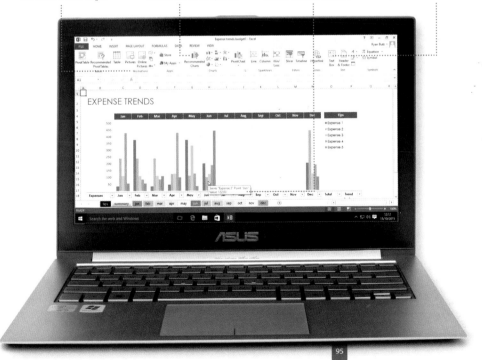

Microsoft PowerPoint

Create and share impressive slide shows for work or for personal use

You'll use it to…

Create a presentation
Start from scratch or use a template

Enter text
Add text to slides and format it

Insert images
Use your own or find clip art online

Use transitions
Add special effects when moving from one slide to the next

Set up animations
Animate objects such as images to add interest to the presentation

Print and export
Share your presentations with other people

Create a presentation

PowerPoint creates slide shows containing text, images and videos, useful for many purposes. Businesses present products and services to customers, teachers present course materials, and families show slides of loved ones on anniversaries and birthdays.

Use a template

As with Word and Excel, PowerPoint has a large collection of templates into which you can drop your text, images and videos. Click File>New and you will see a few of the templates (Fig 1), but most of them are stored online and you must search for them. Enter a word or phrase into the search box or click one of the suggestions below it and the matching templates are displayed. Find one that most closely matches what you need and click it. An

Fig 1 Click File>New to view the templates or start with a blank slide

Fig 2 Take the easy route to presentations and start with one of the many templates

info box is displayed that contains a larger thumbnail image. To see the various slides within a presentation, click the forward and back buttons below the thumbnail image of the slide (Fig 2). When you find a template you like, click the Create button.

Add slides

When you start a new presentation, there may be just one slide or many and it depends on the template that is selected. It is unlikely to be the exact number or type that you need, so click New Slide on the Home tab and choose one of the templates that are displayed. There are several different layouts to choose from. To delete a slide, select it on the left and press the Delete key.

Enter text

Most slide shows contain text, even if it is only the title on the first slide. There are several types of text and the simplest is the text box. Select the Insert tab and click Text Box in the Text section of the ribbon. Click and drag a rectangle on the page to create a text box and a flashing cursor waits for you to type in some text. If you have opened a template, it will contain dummy text to show where the text boxes are located. Click the text, such as the title, delete it and replace it with your own. You can add more text boxes to a slide and delete ones that are not needed.

Text boxes have little squares in the corners and along the sides (handles); click and drag them to resize the text box. As the mouse passes over the edge of a text box, it becomes a cross-shaped arrow and this means the text box can be clicked and dragged to move it on the slide.

Click and drag the top-centre rounded arrow to rotate a text box to the desired angle

Format text

1 Align text Select text and click the left, centre or right align buttons in the ribbon.

2 Set the direction Use the Text Direction button in the ribbon to create vertical text.

3 Set the font Set the font, size, bold and so on in the Font section of the ribbon.

4 Use bullets Bullet lists are perfect for slide shows. Click the button and choose a style.

Microsoft PowerPoint

Apply text effects

There are many effects that can be applied to text and these are accessed by clicking and dragging over some text to select it, right-clicking it and then selecting Format Text Effects from the menu. This opens a panel on the right and there are three buttons near the top. The first is to access Text Fill & Outline, the second is Text Effects and the third is Textbox.

Select Text Fill & Outline and at the bottom of the panel is a button to set the foreground and background colours. The Text Fill options are most useful for large headings and it is possible to have text outlines that are transparent in the middle, a solid or gradient fill, and a picture or pattern fill. Just click a pattern to fill the selected text, for example (Fig 3).

Fig 3 Apply a variety of effects to the text to make it stand out

Rearrange slides
Change the order of the slides by clicking and dragging them up or down the list on the left

Explore the interface
When you need a new slide, click the button and choose from one of the layouts in the template

Arrange objects
Text, images, shapes and other objects can be placed on layers. Click here to change the order

Right-click objects
Right-click everywhere. There are useful hidden menus for text, images, shapes and other objects

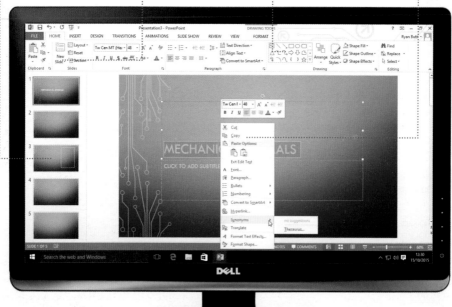

Right-click an image and select Format Picture to apply special effects such as shadows

The Text Effects panel has some eye-catching options that will make headings stand out. Expand the Shadow section and click the Presets button to select one of the ready-made shadow effects. Expand the 3-D Format section and click Top Bevel or Bottom Bevel to make flat text 3D. All the effects can be combined, so you can fill text, add a shadow and make it 3D.

Insert pictures

A slide needs pictures to add interest and there are several sources for them. Select the Insert tab of the ribbon and in the Images section click Pictures to select a photo or artwork from the computer's disk drive, such as a digital camera photo. It is quite likely that the image is too large for the slide, but it is easy to resize them. Click an image to select it and handles (squares) appear in the corners and along the sides. Click and drag a handle to make the image larger or smaller, and click and drag the middle of the image to position it on the slide.

If you don't have any images of your own to accompany your slide show, there is a great collection of clip art and photos online. You can easily search, select images and insert them into slides.

Find images online

1 Select the source Click Online Pictures in the Images section and choose the service to use.

2 Select an image Search Office.com Clip Art and select an image. Click the Insert button.

Animate images

1 Select object Text or images can be animated. Let's animate a photo via the Animations tab.

2 Select effect Click the bottom arrow on the right of the four animations and select one.

3 Set the options This 'Fly In' animation has options and you can select the direction.

4 Set the speed Set the duration (speed) in the ribbon and click Preview on the left.

Print and export

1 Save the slides Select File> Save or Save As and save the presentation source file to disk.

2 Print them Select File>Print and select the number of copies, such as one per person.

3 Set the options There are many options, such as printing notes and the slides per sheet.

4 Export presentation Select File>Export and you can create a PDF file, a video or even a CD.

Many transitions have options, such as the direction of animation when using Push

Select transitions

Transitions are special effects that are often used when moving from one slide to another in the presentation. The next slide could simply appear on the screen, but it might be more interesting if it slides on, slowly fades in while the previous one fades out. Alternatively, the new slide could push out the old one, fade to it through black and any one of a couple of dozen other effects. It is possible to use the same transition effect for the whole slide show or to have a different one for each slide. Try not to use too many or you'll make your audience dizzy with all the effects.

When assigning a transition, there is a Timing section in the ribbon and this enables the duration to be set. A brief duration will produce a fast transition and a long duration slows it down. You can also choose to advance a slide when the mouse is clicked or after a certain time.

View the presentation

So far we have looked at some of the different ways that slides can be created using text, images, animations and transitions. When you have finished all the slides, go to the Slide Show tab of the ribbon to

Preview the slides

1 Play from here To see what a slide will look like, click From Current Slide or From Beginning.

2 Adjust the settings Click on Set Up Slide Show and there are many options, such as continuous looping.

see the options for viewing and setting up slide shows. A slide show can be started from any point and in the Start Slide Show section you'll find buttons to start from the beginning or the currently selected slide.

In the Set Up section of the Slide Show ribbon there is a button to Rehearse Timings. If you are going to give a public presentation or one at work to colleagues or customers, you should practise it until you get it right. You can run through the slides and speech as many times as you need. There is a Record Slide Show button and this enables you to play through the slide show while you narrate it. You will need a microphone in order for PowerPoint to record your speech and you don't have to do it all in one go.

There is more than one way to view a presentation and you could share it online or print it out on paper. Click File and then Print or Export to see the options. Don't forget to set standard or widescreen formats (Fig 4).

Fig 4 Don't forget to set the slide show for standard or widescreen monitors and TVs

Insert a chart
A chart is created by selecting the Insert tab and clicking Chart in the Illustrations section

Pick a style
Each type of chart can be displayed in several different styles. Select one in this list

Change the chart
If you decide that another type of chart would be better, click Change Chart Type in the ribbon

Enter the data
When a chart is inserted, this window is displayed to enable you to enter the data to show

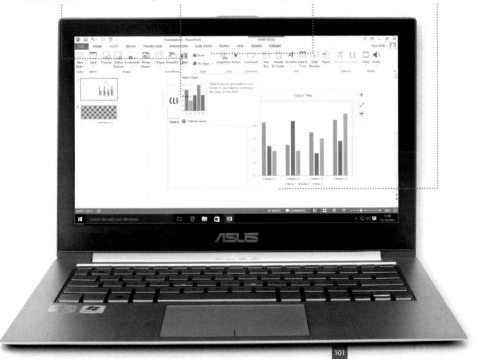

OneDrive

Store files online, to be accessed from anywhere
with an internet connection

You'll use it to…

Store any files
Upload any file regardless of its size

Share with other users
Send uploaded files to others to view
and edit

Edit in OneDrive
Edit photos, videos, documents and files
within OneDrive

Sync with other devices
Access OneDrive from all of your devices

Save storage space
Download only the files you need to access
on OneDrive

Upgrade your storage
Buy as much storage as you need for
your files

Cloud storage on Windows

Since the release of Windows 10, the role and presence of
Microsoft's OneDrive cloud service has changed considerably. It is
no longer an app, as such, and it is more intricately woven into the
very fabric of the operating system, working behind the scenes to
keep your files in sync. Basically, once you log into your Windows
account, OneDrive will be activated.

Accessing your OneDrive

Perhaps the most apparent change to OneDrive is that it no longer
has it's own dedicated app – now it just exists within the File
Manager. That said though, you can still access it quickly by clicking
on the Start menu, choosing the 'All Apps' option and then scrolling
down to 'OneDrive. You can also right-click on the icon to pin it to
your Start screen for easy access (Fig 1). Once open, you can view all
of the files within your OneDrive, create new folders and copy stuff
across by dragging it into the window. The green ticks next to each

Fig 1 You can access your OneDrive from
the Start menu and pin it to your Start
screen for easy access

Fig 2 OneDrive no longer exists as a fancy
app, more a File Manager window through
which you can manage your files

folder signify that the contents have been synced and everything is up to date (Fig 2). You will also notice that the Quick Access options in the top-left corner of the window can be tailored to place key tasks within easy reach. One of which is the option to create a new folder for your OneDrive. When you click on this option a new folder will appear within your OneDrive window that you can re-name and then add files to. It's all relatively straightforward.

Selecting what to sync

In Windows 10, OneDrive utilises a selective sync system, and you can change what gets synced by going to the settings. To do this, right-click on the OneDrive icon in the notification area and then choose the Settings option from the menu. Now click on the 'Choose Folders' tab at the top of the settings window and then click on the option. You can now tick and un-tick the boxes to decide exactly what gets synced and what doesn't.

Web access

All content that is synced to your OneDrive account can be accessed anywhere either by installing the free OneDrive app on your smartphone or tablet device or by using any web browser to log on to **www.onedrive.live.com**. This means that OneDrive provides an effective means of working remotely from the office because all of your synced files are made accessible to you anywhere. And if you make changes to these files and update them, these changes are instantly synced so everything on your OneDrive is as up-to-date as it can be. You'll never be caught short working from old, out of date versions of your files.

You can access your OneDrive anywhere by logging on to **onedrive. live.com** in any browser

OneDrive online apps

1 Log on Go to **onedrive.live. com** to access the web interface of the OneDrive service.

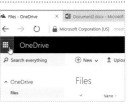

2 Click the icon Now click on the blue grid icon in the top-left corner of the interface.

3 Pick a service You can now choose an app from the selection available.

4 Get creating Now can create new documents or access services like your Calendar.

OneDrive website

When you log onto the OneDrive website to access your files online you will notice that it resembles more of an app-like format with a range of options and information within easy reach. For example, you and view the contents by type in the menu to the left and see exactly how much storage space you have remaining thanks to a heads-up in the lower-left corner.

Fig 3 You can even create new Microsoft Office documents through OneDrive's web interface

Across the top of the window you will see an option to 'Upload' new files and a 'New' menu. Click on this and you will be able to create a new folder to sit within your OneDrive window and even create new Word documents, Excel workbooks, Powerpoint presentations and more office-based options (Fig 3). It goes without saying that any new files that you create will be stored within your

Space remaining
The web version of your OneDrive provides at-a-glance information, such as how much of your allocation is remaining

Create new files
Use this menu to create new folders as well as Microsoft Office documents on the fly

Sort your files
Use this menu to sort and organise your OneDrive files however you see fit, from date modified to ascending and more

Change the view
You can view your OneDrive files as tiles or as a list by clicking on this icon to select the view

Click to select a file in the web interface to bring up options to download, share, move and more

OneDrive and synced whenever changes are made so that the files are kept up-to-date whenever you need to access them.

Remote access

As if OneDrive wasn't a cracking enough service already, it also supports remote access – meaning that you can access any files on your PC from anywhere. To utilise this feature, go to your OneDrive settings screen (see box-out, below) and then under the main 'Settings' tab, tick the 'Let me use OneDrive to fetch any of my files on this PC' option. Once this option has been ticked you can access any of your files remotely from another computer via the OneDrive website, which can prove a life-saver if you need to access a particular file urgently.

When this option has been enabled your connected PC will show up on the OneDrive website and you can access it by logging on to **onedrive.live.com**. If the respective computer is turned on and connected to the internet then you will be able to access any of its folders and files. You can also share files and folders on your OneDrive with other people. To discover how to do this, check out the tutorial to the right.

Access your OneDrive settings

1 Right-click icon Locate the OneDrive icon within your notification area and right-click on it.

2 Choose Settings Click on the Settings option and then use the tabs to navigate the various options.

Share OneDrive files

1 Log on You can only share files from the OneDrive web interface, so log in online.

2 Find file Now locate the folder or file that you want to share and then right-click on it.

3 Share file Select the 'Share' option from the menu and then enter the recipients.

4 Enter details Type in email addresses and notes and then click on the 'Share' button.

Calendar

Organise your time and never miss another appointment, with the Calendar app

You'll use it to...

Create events
Store, scheduled and manage events

Receive alerts
Get notifications direct to your device lock screen

View multiple calendars
Add and select the calendars you use

See national holidays
With Outlook connected, view holiday and lunar calendars

Invite your colleagues
Create events and invite direct from the app

Set recurring events
Set your events to repeat automatically

Ditch the diary

Calendar provides a simple one-place interface for all your calendar and meeting needs (Fig 1). Use it to organise your life across any device signed into your Microsoft account. Create recurring events and invite your email or People contacts to attend.

Managing your life

The Windows 10 Calendar app is an intuitive app that is packed full of features to help you stay organised in your busy working and social lives. The app is intrinsically linked to the Windows 10 Mail app and as such, you can effortlessly switch between the two apps and add accounts so that all of the calendars associated with your various accounts are displayed in the same window (Fig 2). Creating events in the Calendar app is a quick and easy process. You can either click on the date and time within the main calendar window itself or select the 'New event' option from the menu to the left. You can then add in all of the essential details, such as

Fig 1 A simple way to organise your time, and plan events

Fig 2 The 'What's next?' screen is the place to scroll through events in your schedule (when you've planned some

times and locations, as well as invite other people to attend. Once done you can send invites to the attendees and then monitor their interest through the app. Staying organised has never been easier.

Calendar views

There are a variety of different views that you can use to display your calendar, which are accessible from the top of the screen. Here you will find options to view your calendar by Day, Work week (you can select the days of the week you work on in Settings>Calendar Settings), Week, and Month. Click on a view option and the calendar display will instantly change to your preferred view.

Import external calendars

You can import extra calendars into the Calendar app, including from **Outlook.com**. To do this, click on the small cog icon in the lower-left corner and choose Accounts followed by 'Add an account'. Follow the instructions to import your calendar. To remove a calendar, click on the account in the account settings and choose the 'Delete account' option – this doesn't delete any entries from that calendar, but simply removes it from the app. You can choose which calendar to show by selecting Options from Settings.

All of your active accounts will be displayed in the menu to the left of the screen. Click on the arrow next to each account to reveal all of the calendars associated with that account. You can choose to incorporate these into the main calendar window simply by ticking or un-ticking the check boxes next to a calendar. All events associated with a particular calendar will be marked in the main calendar window in the colour of the respective calendar.

Calendar features a weather forecast for the next five days. Go to Settings for more options

Invite guests

1 Create an event Click on a date and time or select the 'New event' option from the menu.

2 Schedule your meeting Before inviting, set a time and date for your meeting.

3 Add more Click on 'More details' and then select the 'invite someone' option.

4 Send invite When you have finished adding details, click on the 'Send' option.

Camera

Follow these simple steps to capture and edit pictures and video on your device

You'll use it to…

Take photographs
Capture and save still images to your device

Record video
Use a compatible camera to capture video

Make quick edits
Crop and rotate still images and trim your video files

Enhance your images
Use enhanced editing features to tune your images

View camera images
View captured images as a slide show on your device

Share your content
Let others see your images and video

Take, edit and share

Using a built-in camera (or compatible connected device), you'll find it easy to capture photos and video. Content is stored locally in the Pictures folder and can be easily viewed and edited direct from the Camera app itself (Fig 1).

Take a simple still image

When you first run the app, it'll request access to your location. Allowing this will let specific sites and applications to reference where the picture was taken: in the case of Facebook, uploaded photographs are map-linked, letting friends see where you were.

With a camera device installed, you should already see an image on the screen. To the right are two button icons: a video camera and stills camera (Fig 2). Let's begin by taking a photo; this is as simple as clicking the camera icon or tapping the screen. You'll see a snap fly off to the left. Swipe up to reveal the action bar before you take a shot, to find a timer (click and click again to set 2, 5 or

Fig 1 Take photos and discover an easy-to-use editing suite, all in one app

Fig 2 The capture interface is incredibly simple: just the icons you need to record the moment

10 seconds) and an exposure slider for low light conditions – these options affect both the camera and video camera.

To access your 'Camera Roll', swipe to the right, or select from the action bar. Continue to swipe to look through your images.

Create a video

It is equally straightforward to capture video. Click the video camera icon to start recording – the elapsed time appears in the lower left corner. When you are ready to stop recording, click the icon again (you'll see the elapsed time fly off to the left). A useful feature is the ability to take snapshots as a video is recording: to do this, simply tap the screen.

1 Quick video trimming Grab video timeline handles and drag to set new start and end points.

Discover simple editing

Select a photograph from your Camera Roll and swipe/right-click for the action bar. Perhaps most importantly, this is the place to find 'Delete'. But you will also find options to view the picture in a supporting application (such as Photos), set the picture as your lock screen, and view the roll as a 'Slideshow'. On the right are options to Rotate, Crop and Edit. Rotate will turn the image through 90 degrees with each click. Crop will set a grid over the photo which can be manipulated to select a specific area – you can also change the aspect ratio from a series of defaults.

The final option – Edit – is the place to discover a whole series of tools. Of the basic fixes, Straighten will help you level a scene, Red Eye will restore colour to pupils, and Retouch will remove blemishes and marks based on detail around the error itself. Experiment with the editing categories – any changes you make can be reversed or saved with options on the action bar.

2 Try out Retouch From Edit> Basic Fixes, click the picture to remove unsightly marks.

3 Swipe to share Click Share in the top bar to select an app that can publish your images.

Use the Crop function to select a specific portion of your photo and alter the aspect ratio

4 Select a different viewer Pick 'Open with' from the action bar and choose an application.

Photos

Photos

The Photos app collates all of your images from your local machine or OneDrive account into one intuitive interface

You'll use it to…

View existing photos
Quickly access photos via collections or albums

OneDrive access
You can access images from your OneDrive Account

Share photos
Share your photos via Social Networks or email

Edit photos
Use the built-in editor to jazz up your photos

Import photos
Import Photos from your camera, memory card or phone

Change Tile photo
Customise the Windows Start Tile for launching the Photos app

Source photos automatically

By default the Photos app automatically scans your local Pictures folder or OneDrive account (online storage) for photos and videos. It then organises the contents into Collections and Albums (Fig 1) where you can then view, share or Edit the photos – by adding effects or filters and more.

Access your Photos

By default once you launch the Photos app you are taken to the top-left Collection option. From here any photos located will be displayed and organised based on date taken. Photos could include those imported from other devices or when you press the 'Prt Scr' key to take a screenshot. In order to view a photo just click on it, but note the options at the top, which we will talk about later (Fig 2). However if you have a lot of photos to wade through a useful tip is to select the date header at the top of a Collection and this will

Fig 1 The Photos app automatically scans both local and online sources for any Photos/videos you have

Fig 2 When you select a photo to view, you have several options at the top for managing it

enable you access a range of months to speed up the selection process. Alongside the Collection you also have Albums and this option includes a Camera roll and a dedicated Screenshots folder. Clicking on an Album will then showcase the images.

Add a folder

You can manage where the Photos app looks for content. Select the bottom Settings icon and look for the option called Sources. Beneath this will be the default locations where the app looks for

the photos, you can simply click the x to remove a location or you can use 'Add a folder'. This will enable you to browse your computer for a specific folder to source images from.

Add and manage albums

The app also organises groups of Photos into Albums, but you can adjust these to taste. From the interface select Albums and then pick an album by clicking on the large thumbnail. You will then find a cover photo, alongside the date header beneath. You can either delete the album via the 'Remove album' icon at the top-right or change the cover photo by clicking on the Edit pencil icon. The Date field box will then be highlighted and you can click on this to edit the title to something more meaningful. Likewise you can click on 'Change cover' to select a suitable replacement from the other photos in that Album. When you have finished just select the Done tick icon. Alternatively you can create your own album from scratch. Simply head back to Albums and then click the '+' symbol at the top-right. You then have to browse through the sourced photos and keep clicking on the ones you want to add to the album. Then add a suitable title and cover photo as per above.

Head to the Settings>Tile option to set a custom photo for the Windows Start Tile

Creating an Album

1 New Album Click the Albums option and then select the '+' icon at the top of the page.

2 Select Photos Select the photos you want by clicking on them and tap the tick to finish.

3 Add Title Input a title or click on 'Change cover' to adjust the large cover photo.

4 Save the Album When you are finished click on the Save icon at the top to view the album.

Edit photos

By default the Photos app will automatically turn on Auto-enhance mode, which can either change the photo from a perspective point of view or adjust the exposure levels to improve on the original. This does not necessarily mean you want the enhancement. Thankfully you can toggle this option on or off quickly. If you select a photo you will see a wand like icon at the top. Clicking on this will allow you to switch between the Auto-enhance mode. Additionally you can select the pencil Edit icon to enter the main editing tools. From here all of your basic fixing options are displayed to the left and right side of the photo (Fig 3). On the left side you can choose Filters and then pick from a list of thumbnail/filter options such as black and white on the right. You can select a filter to get a real-time

Fig 3 The Photos app has an editing option to adjust any selected photo

Sharing your photo
The top left Share icon can be used to share the photo via social network accounts such as Twitter or via your Mail app

Run a Slideshow
If either a Collection or Album has multiple photos included you can use the Slideshow function to browse through them automatically

Range of Editing options
You have a range of editing options open to you via the pencil Edit icon or the Enhance icon

More icon
The top-right more icon '...' will allow you to print the photo and also open it up in third party software like Adobe Photoshop

 You can use Cortana
to instantly find photos
from a particular time by
speaking your selection

preview of what it does. If you head back to the Basic Fixes option
you can then select on the right the Crop tool, which will allow you
to drag the circular corners with your mouse to re-size the photo.
Don't worry if you make a mistake whilst editing as you can click the
'x' icon to cancel or the tick/save icon to implement the changes.

Import photos

The Photos app also has a useful Import function that allows you to
import Photos from a range of additional sources. This could include
memory cards, USB sticks and even Smartphones (the iPhone is also
supported). You can access the Import feature via the Collection
menu to the left of the interface. All you need to do next is ensure
that your device, memory stick or Smartphone is plugged in (wait
until the OS has installed the drivers for it) and then click on the
top right Import icon. The software will now scan the source for
compatible photos and once found it will display how many – with
the option to delete the contents from the source after importing.
You can then choose Import to add all the photos. The small tutorial
below will quickly run through the steps to give you additional
insight into this feature.

Import photos

1 Insert Device
First plug in the device to the
computer to source the photos.

2 Import process
Now select Collection and choose
Import from the right to begin.

Share multiple photos

1 Choose which photos Click
on Collection or Albums and
navigate to a group of photos.

2 Select icon Now click on the
Select icon via the very top of
the page.

3 Multiple clicks Next keep
clicking on the photos you want
to include.

4 Share the photos Finally click
on the top Share icon to choose
how you want to share.

Groove Music

Groove Music is a streamlined app that allows you to listen to your favourite music

You'll use it to…

Listen to music
Listen to your favourite music tracks on your PC

Multi device support
Music added to One Drive can be accessed across all your devices

File format support
Groove supports a range of file formats including flac and mp3

Create playlists
Customise your tracks into playlists for enhanced listening

Cortana integration
Control your music playback with the power of your voice

Groove Music Pass
Tap into a subscription based service to stream/download millions of tracks

Fig 1 Groove Music will scan your PC automatically for compatible music

Fig 2 You can change the location where Groove looks for music

Get your Groove on

Groove Music is an app that allows you to play music that has been gleamed from a variety of sources (Fig 1). This can include the Groove Music Pass streaming service (similar to Spotify), imported music from iTunes, the Windows Store or even music added to your OneDrive account from other Windows 10 devices you own.

Change music location

When you first start Groove Music it will automatically scan and add music that it finds in your computers default music folder. However you can adjust where the app looks for music. The first point of call is to ensure that you have signed-in with your Microsoft account, this should be automatic, but if not click on Sign-in at the base, as this will help sync all your music and settings to the cloud. Next you will want to select the Settings icon at the base and from here look for the header 'Music on this PC' and then directly beneath click on the option 'Choose where we look for music'. At this point you can

click on the '+' icon to browse for a new location on your PC, for example C:\EpicMusic and choose 'Add this folder to music' (Fig 2). When you have finished you can click Done. Alternatively you can use the 'x' icon next to a folder to remove it before using Done, but note the music won't be deleted, just the search location.

Play your music

Once the music is in your library you'll find in the top left corner a Search bar, Albums, Artists, Songs or Now playing menu choices for navigating to your music. For arguments sake if you click on Albums you can then select an album cover to reveal its track list. Once you have found a song just click on the track name and use the Play icon to start the music. You can also manipulate the music via the playback controls at the base.

Create playlists

In Groove Music you can create playlists of your favourite tracks. There are a number of ways to create playlists, however the most obvious method can be found via the left-hand menu. Select the '+ New Playlist' icon and then give your playlist a suitable name like MyTracks. Once the playlist is created it will appear in the list below and the next step is to add tracks to it. You can do this quickly by right clicking on a track name or an album thumbnail image and choosing 'Add to'. A side menu will then appear allowing you to select the previously created playlist. When you choose the 'Add to' option there is a sub-option that enables you to create a new playlist. When you add a track to a playlist you can quickly click the top right notification to view the tracks in the new playlist or alternatively select the playlist from the left menu.

You can add tracks from one playlist to another by selecting the playlist and using the 'Add to' option

Managing playlists

1 Your Playlist First select one of your created playlist's from the left menu.

2 Select icon From the resulting screen click on the Select icon to the right of the interface.

3 Choose your track Now select a track by clicking on the small box to the side.

4 Management options To adjust the track order, remove it or save to listen offline.

Utilise OneDrive

OneDrive is tied to your Microsoft account and by default it offers the ability to store and access data online. However the beauty of Groove Music is that it will also allow you to tap into the same online storage for adding music. This benefits you more if you have multiple devices with the same Microsoft account attached because it means that music you add to OneDrive can then be accessed from your Windows Mobile, tablet and even the Xbox One. Thus, no matter which device you own you can download or stream the music; something which you have to pay a subscription for with third party services such as iTunes Match. To add music to your OneDrive account you can either upload tracks to a dedicated Music folder using a web browser (**www.onedrive.com**) or via the

Fig 3 You can filter your music to display content from a particular source

Groove Music Pass
A Groove Music Pass is a subscription based service that allows access to millions of tracks

Music on this PC
The 'Music on this PC' header option allows you to adjust the folder location where Groove Music sources music from

Downloads
The Downloads toggle enables you to automatically download music to your computer from the store – even if it was purchased on another device

Missing album art
The Media Info toggle is useful to enable as Groove Music will automatically attempt to restore any missing album art for each track/album

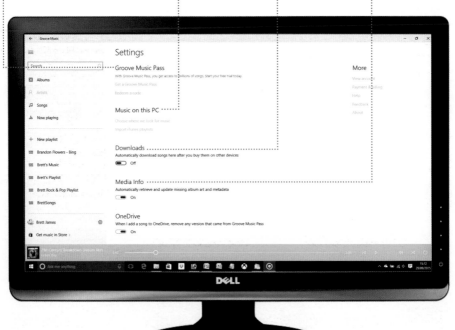

If you head to Settings you can change the apps default background theme colour

computer itself. By default a folder is added to your PC under this location 'C:\Users\Username\OneDrive\Music'. So as long as you paste music into here it will upload it for other devices to access. All changes are synced, so if you delete content from one source it reflects on the other. You can also filter music so it only displays content from OneDrive. In Artists, for example, click on the All option under the Filter header and select 'On OneDrive' (Fig 3).

Cortana support

When you play music playback controls appear at the base of the interface or if you minimise the app you also get a smaller mini player pop-up when you adjust the volume. Likewise you can hover your mouse over the Groove Music icon on the taskbar to get controls as well. However there is also another option to explore in the form of Cortana. The virtual digital assistant can be used to play tracks, pause or forward between tracks, as well as to play playlists. In order to get Cortana to work just speak the phrase "Hey Cortana" and then follow this with "Play", "Pause", "Skip Forward" or "Skip back" for general playback controls or be more specific and experiment with asking for specific songs or artists.

Play music with Cortana

1 Get Cortana's attention Start by saying "Hey Cortana... Play song, by artist name".

2 Pause playback Now just say "Hey Cortana... Pause" and restart by saying "Hey Cortana...Play".

Pin to Start

1 Pick your track Select either an Album or a track that you want to pin.

2 Context Menu Now Right-click the track or Album cover and choose 'Pin to Start'.

3 View in Start Next open up the Start Menu and look for the new Pin.

4 Group name You can now click the pin to play or why not add more pins and create a group.

Films & TV

Watch movies, television shows and your own digital camera and phone videos

You'll use it to…

Download movies
Get the latest movies and download them

Download TV series
Get top television series to watch any time

Get free content
Download movie trailers and free TV shows

Browse your videos
Explorer videos you have transferred to the PC

Play your videos
Watch videos taken on digital cameras and phones

Watch anywhere
Watch TV shows and movies on any device

Watch TV and movies

Films & TV enables you to download and watch the best movies on your computer or other Windows 10 devices you own. Get top rated television shows and even whole series, and watch them anytime and anywhere.

Your entertainment centre

The Films & TV app is likely to be one of the most used on your computer and it is a home entertainment centre where you can download and watch great movies including the latest Hollywood blockbusters, and you can also watch TV programmes and catch up on series you have missed. Instead of renting DVDs, you can buy content online and watch it on your computer, other Windows 10 devices, and even your connected television in the lounge.

The content for Films & TV can be purchased using the Store app and the two work together to buy and play items. Links in the app take you to the Store and when you return, the items you

Fig 1 Browse your purchased and free movies and TV shows using Films & TV

Fig 2 Watch your own videos that have been transferred to your computer from your phone or camera

purchased are there ready to watch. A few items in the Store are free, such as film trailers and pilots for TV series. You can also browse and watch your own movies after they have been transferred to the computer and stored in the Videos folder. It is a great app.

Stream movies

Movies and TV shows can be watched in two different ways. They can be downloaded and stored on the computer or they can be streamed. Streaming plays the media over the internet and it starts in a few seconds without having to be downloaded first, but if you download the film or TV programme, it can be watched without an internet connection in offline mode. Use the filter on the home screen to show streamed or downloaded items.

Find films and shows

There is nothing to watch when Films & TV is first run. All it contains are links to the Store and a few promoted items. Your first task is to explore the films, TV programmes and series that are available and to purchase some.

A small number of items are free, so use these to familiarise yourself with the app and to try out the features. The free content may change over time, but browsing sections in the Store like Sales and Specials will usually turn up a few items.

Films & TV is integrated with the Store app. Select Films or TV in the menu on the left and click 'Shop for more' in the bottom left corner of the app. The Store app takes over and you can then browse the items. Before purchasing a movie from the Store, look for the Trailer link on the item's page. Click it to stream it and watch it. Then if you like it, click the button to buy it or click the Free icon.

Look for the Trailers link and you can preview movies before you buy them

Get free programmes

1 Open the app Open Films & TV and click 'Shop for more' in the bottom left corner.

2 Browse the Store Use the categories to browse the store and find something you like.

3 View the details Click an item in the store to go to the details page, like this one.

4 Own it Scroll down and the pilot episode is free. Click it to own it.

Own movies and TV

Free Films and TV shows in the Store have a Free button and clicking it and it changes it to Owned, which might lead you to wonder what next? Purchasing a movie or TV programme in the Store has the same effect. There are some extra steps because you need to enter payment information, but the end result is the same and you own the item once you have completed the purchase.

Anything you own can be played on any computer or device running Windows 10 that you own, provided you sign in using your Microsoft account. You could buy a film or TV programme on one computer and watch it on another for instance. This is one reason why nothing happens when you buy something or grab a freebie. Another reason why downloads are not automatic is because of

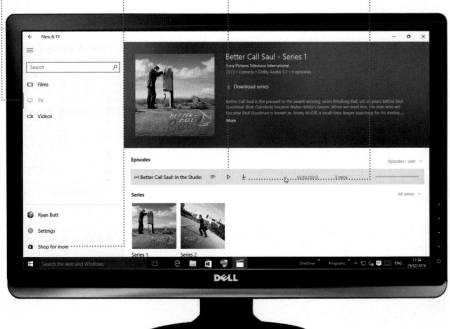

Fig 3 Click the link on the right to show episodes you own or all episodes available

Pick a category
What do you want to watch? Click TV, Film or Videos to show items in those categories

To the Shop
Switch to the Store app to browse for more TV shows and films to add to your collection

Play it
Stream the film or TV show or play it from disk, depending on whether it is downloaded

Download it
This item has not been downloaded. Click this button to save it to disk and play it offline

Click the information button to display a pop-up panel with a complete description

the large amount of disk space required for long movies in high resolution. Open Films & TV, select Films or TV in the left panel and click a movie or show. Click an item and click Play or Download. If you Play without downloading it, it is streamed, but if you download it first then it is played from the disk drive.

Resolution and space

Movies and TV programmes are available in standard definition (SD) or high definition (HD) and a choice is displayed when you click the download button in Film & TV. SD content looks fine on small screens and it has the advantage of smaller and faster downloads that require less disk space. More SD movies and shows can be stored on the disk drive than with HD.

HD resolution content is the better quality of the two and images are sharper. This is particularly noticeable on large screens if you view content on a big screen TV for instance. The disadvantages include longer and larger downloads, and more disk space is required to store each item. Fewer movies and shows can be stored on the disk drive. Also be aware that some ISPs place download limits at peak times of the day.

Manage your media

1 Select the resolution Click a download link and you have a choice of SD or HD.

2 Remove watched content Struggling for disk space? Click Remove all to delete watched items.

Play your own movies

1 Transfer your videos Transfer your digital camera and phone videos to the Videos folder.

2 Films & TV Start Films & TV and select Videos on the left to browser your home videos.

3 Open folders Click folders to open them and click the arrow top left to go back.

4 Watch videos Click a video to view it. Click the double headed arrow for full-screen view.

Xbox app

Windows 10 integrates Xbox Live services into the platform and the Xbox app is a key part of this

You'll use it to...

Keep track of Achievements
View Windows 10, Xbox 360 and Xbox One achievements via the app

Manage Friends list
Add or manage existing friends and view their online status

Capture gameplay
Capture PC gameplay and screenshots

Launch games
The app can tap into third party titles to launch and play games

Stream games or TV
You can stream Xbox One Games or TV to your Windows 10 PC/Tablet

Edit gameplay
Perform basic editing on your gameplay videos

Fig 1 If you own an Xbox One you will get more out of the app

Fig 2 The Home screen allows you to view recently played players so you can add them as friends

Windows 10 Xbox app

The Xbox app is the central hub for tapping into the services of Xbox live. In fact if you have an Xbox One you can stream games and TV (with a compatible card) from the latter to your Windows 10 PC/tablet (Fig 1). The app also allows you to track achievements, view a friend's list and capture or edit PC game play.

Home screen

With the Xbox app you need to sign-in with a Microsoft account, preferably one attached to an Xbox One. Once you have logged in you are taken to the Home screen with your recently played games on the left. There is also a list of featured games that you can click on to download from the Store. To the right is your Activity feed, this populates in real-time – more so if you have friends or follow games and people. From the latter you'll be able to view recent achievements, who's added who as a friend or add and view comments. You can add your own comments by using the

input field-box at the base of each discussion. Directly to the right is where you can view your existing friends and see if they are online. You can also use the drop-down box next to where it says Friends (Fig 2) to browse people you have recently played against.

Your profile

Alongside the Home screen you can click on your profile icon via the top-left (it displays your gamer score and an existing Avatar image). From the resulting screen you get more of a personalised look at your activity, plus the tabs at the top can be clicked on to view achievements, any game play captured and who you are following. If you click on the Customise tab at the top you can adjust your Avatar, but this does involve downloading an Avatars app from the store.

Following people or games

It can be difficult to add friends from scratch, but thankfully if you click the Home icon the app will suggest people it thinks you should be friends with. Beneath this is a 'See more' icon, which you can click on to expand the available choices. If you want to add a friend this is a two step process – if you add a friend they simply become someone you follow unless that person confirms your request. If you are unsure whether to add someone, simply click on their thumbnail picture, this will enable you to view their profile so you can see if they share common interests such as the games you play. If you want to then add them the option 'Add friend' will appear above their profile. Once the friend is added their feed will start displaying on the Home screen. If you click on a game, from your Achievements menu, you have the option to Follow it too.

Use the menu on the left-hand side to jump straight to your Achievements

Find people

1 Find input box Click on the Home icon and then select the 'Find people' input box.

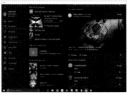

2 Search on Xbox Live Now type in a name, such as 'e' and click on the magnifying icon.

3 View Profile Next select the Profile>Achievements tab to see what games they like to play.

4 Add Friend Once you are happy click on 'Add friend' then click on OK to confirm it.

Gameplay capture

The Xbox app allows you to capture gameplay and screenshots from your PC games. This can include arcade style games from the Store, as well as third party titles from Steam. Basically you head to the My Games menu and inside here all your games will be listed or you can click 'Add a game from your PC' to include third party compatible titles. Once you have your game it's worth checking out the bottom Settings>Game DVR tab. From here you can toggle the Background recording to on and then adjust everything from quality settings to the time you can record footage for. Now return to the My Games section and select a game to play. With the game running you can then press and hold Win+G to bring up the Game bar (Fig 3). With this you can then take screenshots,

Fig 3 The Game bar allows you to take screenshots or record gameplay

Capture quality
You can adjust the Video encoding to improve the capture quality, but again this can impact on the PC performance

Record that
Similar to the Xbox One you can set the app to record footage taken from the last 30-seconds to up to ten minutes

Run in the background
You can enable the Game DVR function to run in the background while you are playing games; though this can impact on PC performance

Longer clips
You can also set the main Clip recording time, so when you bring up the Game bar (Win+G) it will allow up to two hours of recording

You can also use an Xbox One controller – attached to the PC – to bring up the Game bar

capture up to the last ten minutes of gameplay or two hours of continuous gameplay. With the latter it will display a red indicator in the top right corner to show its working. You can hide this by pressing Win+T. When you have finished recording just bring back the Game bar and press the Stop button. Afterwards you can view the recording by selecting the Xbox app's Game DVR menu and 'On this PC' tab.

Stream games from Xbox One

If you have an Xbox One you can stream games or TV programmes (via the OneGuide menu if you have a Digital TV card) to your Windows 10 PC/tablet. However for games you must ensure that both your PC/tablet are on the same network. Also on the Xbox One you need to head to Settings>Preferences to enable the streaming. Once this is done head to the Xbox app's Connect menu option and then choose your console that you want to connect to. Once its established connection you can use the More option to disconnect or use the Stream tab to stream from the Xbox One. Alternatively you can select a game from your Achievements menu and choose 'Play from console' to stream directly.

Streaming in action

1 Stream your game With the console/controller connected select a game and choose 'Play from console'.

2 Improve stream performance Once connected select the top right icon to adjust the stream quality.

Edit gameplay footage

1 Game DVR menu From the Xbox App select the Game DVR menu option.

2 Choose game clips Now click the Everything drop-down and choose Game clips.

3 Trim footage Select your Game clip and then under the preview window choose Trim.

4 Trim & Save Using the sliders you can now trim the start and end points. Choose Save copy.

News

With news from multiple sources, it's easy to stay up to date as it happens, with News

You'll use it to…

Get the latest news
See stories from multiple sources in one place

Personalise news content
Choose the news sources you want to see

Add your favourite feeds
Bring RSS feeds directly into the app

View content by country
Have News show stories from around the world

See foreign language content
Search by language to view selected international publications

Glance at the latest
The News live tile will quickly show what's new

Fig 1 The News live tile will cycle through the latest stories automatically

Fig 2 (Right) Scroll across the app to discover new stories within the various news sections

Read all about it

Whether your passion is sport, technology or politics, News will gather together stories from numerous sources worldwide into one simple application. The app's scrolling live tile will also display updates direct to your Start menu (Fig 1).

Navigate the news

When you first open News, you'll discover the default collection of news sections across the top of the screen. More content can be accessed by clicking on the menu in the top-left corner and then choosing the Interests section (Fig 2). The Search News dialogue resides in the top-right corner; use it to find a recent story, current news or research a historical topic.

Browsing through the default news sections, you will discover 'In Pictures' and 'Video' news – sections that draw on more modern visual content, made possible by the worldwide web. The In Pictures section in particular, often features quite thought-provoking images.

At the bottom of the feature story you'll see the time at which news stories were last updated. Swipe up or right-click to reveal the action bar and use the Refresh button (lower right) to update.

Adding news

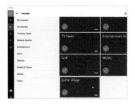

Get specific content

If you're particularly interested in a subject or field, you can view related content as a Topic. Multiple topics can be displayed in your application feed and as live tiles on the Start screen. To create a topic, select Interests from the menu at the far left of the app. Select the '+' and enter a subject of your choosing; relevant content will then be displayed as with any other section.

See news as you want

You can easily customise the news sections and content displayed by the News application. We have already explained how you can add to your personal Interests by selecting the option from the menu. But you can explore topics relating to any type of news and then add them by clicking on the '+' icon (after which it will turn into a tick). You can also get local news beamed to your PC, but to do this you have to grant the app permission to use your location. You can select Local news from the menu by clicking on this category, after which all of the breaking headlines from your area will be relayed to your news feed. Finally, news items with accompanying video footage will also be accessible from their own 'Videos' section within the menu. Go here if you want a little extra visual entertainment with your news feeds. Ultimately, everything is also accessible by scrolling across the top of the News interface, so the news that you crave is always within easy reach when you want to read it.

1 Go to Interests From the main menu, select 'Interests' and this will list the various news topics.

2 Select a new topic Browse the list of available topics and then click one that interests you.

3 Add the topic Click on the '+' icon and it will be added to your feed and turn into a tick.

4 Jump to topic Scroll to the topic at the top of the app and click on it to jump there.

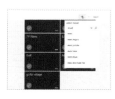

You can easily customise the news sections and content displayed by the application

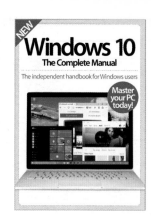

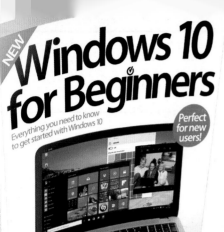

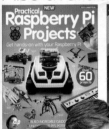